This book is dedicated to all seekers of truth.

✳ ✳ ✳

Jehovah's Witnesses under the leadership of the Watchtower Bible & Tract Society of New York now have approaching 6,000,000 active members. The birth of this worldwide movement can be traced back to its humble beginnings as "The International Bible Students Association" started by Charles Taze Russell in 1881. Their beliefs have undergone many revisions during the last century and presently reject many of the fundamental beliefs of mainstream Christianity, believing that only 144,000 will go to heaven, while all others who earn salvation will live forever on earth. The members of the Governing Body of this sect believe themselves to be God's only channel of communication with humans.

The membership claim to be "separate from the world" and avoid all involvement in politics, while discouraging higher education and the pursuit of secular success. They believe themselves to be God's chosen people and believe that the Biblical promises made to Israel are being fulfilled upon them, as they are a modern-day spiritual Israel. Their mission is to persuade you to join them and avoid the penalty of death, when the present world system ends at the imminent battle of Armageddon.

OPENING THE DOOR

to
Jehovah's
Witnesses

Trevor Willis

PINPOINT PUBLICATIONS
WORTHING

OPENING THE DOOR
to Jehovah's Witnesses

First published in 2001 by
PINPOINT PUBLICATIONS,
6 Broadwater Way, Broadwater,
Worthing, West Sussex, BN14 9LP.
Telephone 01903 232346

Letters sent to the publisher will be forwarded to the author.
To obtain further copies of this book please telephone
the publisher for further information.

ISBN 0-9540182-0-6

Printed and bound in the UK by
CREATIVE PRINT AND DESIGN,
Ebbw Vale, Wales.

Designed by Cecil Smith
Typeset in 10/12 Palatino and Garamond by
EVERGREEN GRAPHICS,
11 The Drive, Craigweil on Sea
Aldwick, West Sussex PO21 4DU.
MEMBERS OF THE GUILD OF MASTER CRAFTSMEN

CONTENTS

INTRODUCTION   xi

1   *THE KNOCK ON YOUR DOOR*   1

The First Call   1
The Attraction   2
Contagious Enthusiasm   3
Provoking Response   5
The Call that Changed my Life   7
Door to Door   9

2   *INSIDE THE CONGREGATION*   11

Meetings   11
Will You Join the Dance?   12
Baptism   14
Obedience   16
Running Ahead   17
Will You Walk a Little Faster?   19
A Woman's Place   20
Assemblies   21
Reaching Out   21

3   *BUYING OUT THE TIME*   23

Life at School   23
Pioneering   27
Careers   30
Marriage and Children   32
Under Pressure   33

4   *KEEPING SEPARATE FROM THE WORLD*   35

Workmates   35
Friends in the Congregation   35
Relatives   37
The Pool of Tears   39

5 *LATE FOR A VERY IMPORTANT DATE*   47

Pastor Russell's Society – 1887 to 1917   47
Judge Rutherford Takes Charge   51

6 *THE DORMOUSE GOES INTO THE TEAPOT*   53

Punished For Falling Asleep – 1917 to 1925   53
No Heaven for the Righteous   57
The Same Promise   58

7 *A NEW NATION*   61

Claim to Fame – 1925 to 1960   61
The Nation Needs Laws   64
The Advantages of Hindsight   65
The Faithful and Discreet Slave   65
A Name For the New Nation   66
Jehovah not Jesus   67
The Great Crowd   68
Prison Bonds   70
Bethsarim   71
World War II   72

8 *PAINTING THE ROSES*   75

The Divine Purpose – 1960 to 1990   75
The Time has Come   76
Disappointed Again   79
This Generation   84

9 *ALL EAGER FOR THE TREAT*   89

1990 – 2000 – and Beyond   89
Jerusalem and – 607 BCE   93
A Crisis of Conscience   94
Is Sincerity Enough?   98
Accurate Knowledge   98
Inaccurate Knowledge   99
Off With Their Heads!   99

10 *THE WITNESSES' OWN BIBLE*   101

Who is the Word?   104
The Name Over Every Name   105
Prove These Things for Yourselves   109

11 *NO PART OF THE WORLD*   111

Voting   111
Stop Press – change of policy   114
All the Benefits   115
Mind Control   116
The Watchtower Society's Armageddon   117

12 *PAGAN CELEBRATIONS*   123

Birthdays   123
Christmas   124
Not Commanded to Celebrate Christ's Birth   125
Pagan Customs that are accepted   126
Enter the Spider   127

13 *RESPECT FOR BLOOD*   131

Human Blood   132
Blood Transfusion   132
The Lord's Supper   137
To Watch is enough   138

14 *UNDERSTANDING JEHOVAH'S WITNESSES*   139

The Wall   141
Opening the Door   142

15 *SUMMARY*   147

Careers   147
Opinions   147
Cold Canvassing   147
No Heaven   148
The Watchtower Bible & Tract Society   148
Jehovah Not Jesus   148
Friends and Relatives   148
Conditions of Membership   149
No Holy Communion   149
No Other Christians   149

16 *CONCLUSION*   151

Knowledge is light and banishes darkness.
Seekers of truth desire to be fully informed.
The experience and opinions of those
Who have walked a path before you,
Should not be seized upon as belief
Or a shortcut to understanding.
At the same time it would be unwise
To disregard their sincere testimony.

✳ ✳ ✳

INTRODUCTION

With few exceptions, most people have come in contact with Jehovah's Witnesses. They arouse feelings ranging from admiration and curiosity to intense annoyance. As people search for truth and meaning in life, the Witnesses' ready-made package can appear to be the answer. Their claim is that they alone have

"the truth."

It is important to realize the difference between the
Watchtower Bible and Tract Society
and Jehovah's Witnesses.

The Society is the legally registered corporation for Jehovah's Witnesses. They have branches which double as printing plants all around the world and they live in these **Bethel Homes.** The main headquarters are in New York. The Society make all decisions and decide doctrine, rules and policy. No accounts are shown to the ordinary members.

Although these men also call themselves Jehovah's Witnesses, they lead and are in charge, they have referred to themselves collectively as God's prophet. They are responsible for the claims and accusations that appear in the literature they produce. Throughout this book, the Watchtower Society is referred to as "they" rather than the impersonal "it."

The name Jehovah's Witnesses refers to the many people who make up the congregations around the world - the membership. They will often be referred to as Witnesses. To become a Witness is relatively easy. To become a member of the Watchtower

Society is far harder and can only be achieved by appointment. Very few are asked to join. The highest rank is appointment as a member of the **Governing Body**. These men manipulate all Bible texts and decide how to apply them to Jehovah's Witnesses. They are responsible for the changes that have taken place in their teachings over the years.

The average rank and file Jehovah's Witness is in a different category. Most of them are sincere people, who have in many cases been attracted to the movement by a genuine desire to understand the Bible and serve God as best they can. They are often very kind people who have become unwittingly involved. Their distant and sometimes hostile attitude towards those outside the movement is a result of what the Society term "mental regulating," in the form of books, magazines, lectures, question and answer discussions and private counselling – coupled with a fear of expulsion if they associate with anyone who their Society see as a threat to their cause.

Most members would show a great deal more empathy if they were not actively encouraged to view all outsiders as sinners who are about to be killed by the God they love. After many years in the movement and being trained to view all outsiders with suspicion, believing that they are a threat to their salvation, it is inevitable that some Witnesses have lost a great deal of their feeling towards people who are not part of their organization.

Despite the movement's worldwide growth, few independent books have been written about them. Most encyclopaedias give some facts and there are some pamphlets in circulation, although even these are not readily available. This is surprising considering the phenomenal output of literature in over 132 languages produced by The Watchtower Bible & Tract Society. Naturally all such literature is designed to promote them in the most favourable light possible. There are however many areas of the movement that their current literature does not fully explain.

- **What did their Society originally believe?**
- **How did Jehovah's Witnesses come to hold their present beliefs?**

- **What is it like to be a member?**
- **How do they view those outside their organization?**
- **How do their beliefs differ from mainstream Christianity?**

This book covers all aspects of the movement going back to their beginnings and showing how their present beliefs evolved and why so many changes have been necessary. Few Witnesses are aware how many changes have taken place or how different the originally held beliefs were. Each new set of beliefs has been labelled "the truth." Witnesses refer to themselves as being in "the truth" and refer to their movement as "the truth."

Unlike other Bible based religions, the Witnesses claim to understand the intended meaning of every verse of scripture. Their Society claims to be God's sole channel of communication to humans with a special ability to interpret scripture. They claim to be the only true Christians in the world. As you will see their beliefs set them apart from Christendom Christians collectively.

Their one-dimensional outlook puzzles many who have spoken with Jehovah's Witnesses. The Witness mind seems impervious to all outside influence. You may have relatives who are Witnesses or you may just be curious about their beliefs. If you are unaware of the methods used to draw people into the Watchtower Society, you could unwittingly become involved yourself. To be forewarned is to be forearmed.

Every time a Witness knocks on your door you are open to persuasion. If the Witnesses have "the truth" this could be a good thing, if not, you should be aware of the steps that lead to becoming a Witness and the beliefs and outlook you would need to adopt.

You may ask why I feel qualified to write about Jehovah's Witnesses.

I was born and raised a strict Witness by a mother and father who have now spent forty years in the movement. My father has been an **elder** for most of that time. I was appointed as a **pioneer** – the term for a full time door-to-door evangelist. To leave the movement, as I did at almost thirty, is no small achievement. A lifetime of conditioning was only overcome by an intensive study of the Society's entire history and a soul-searching reflection on the meaningfulness of continuing as a Jehovah's Witness, in the light of the knowledge I came to possess.

Those who know little of the powerful influence exerted over its members by the Society will find it difficult to appreciate how painful it was to leave behind an entire way of life, then live among the very people I had been trained to view as "bad association" and instructed to avoid on any social level. Perhaps harder still to go against my entire family and be viewed by them as evil.

It may seem foolish in the first place to believe that by being a Witness I would live forever on earth and never experience old age or death, while all people not belonging to the sect would be destroyed. This though is the hope of all members. Such are the methods used to persuade those that become involved that they come to believe this and live their entire lives in anticipation. What chance do the children have?

I find myself disturbed by parents who are Witnesses, that make their children read books favourable to their Society, but forbid them from reading anything independently written about their Society.

You will find this book both factual and informative while containing a flavour of personal experience. I have tried to be fair, but having left the movement after seeing its flaws, it is impossible not to show some bias and is therefore critical rather than sympathetic. This offers an alternative to the vast amount of publicity material produced by the Witnesses own publishing company, which you are frequently offered at your door and are of course free to read as well.

Very few Witnesses are open minded enough to read anything written about them by anyone other than their own organization. They know that to do so is heavily frowned upon as it is said to show a lack of faith. This is bound to rob them of the opportunity of developing a balanced viewpoint. The Watchtower Society discourages the reading of all other religious material as well. This is surprising in view of the vast number of quotations found in their own publications. The writers at the Bethel printing plants must spend considerable time reading such material themselves.

The material in the chapters ahead explains why some members have not found the Society's ready-made answers fully satisfying. If they have "the truth" then reading another viewpoint cannot harm them. Naturally their Society would rather their members read only their own favourable books. The sense of loss and disappointment a member can feel, if he or she leaves, can be immense and has led many to experience nervous breakdowns and some to commit suicide. One of the greatest ways to combat such depression is to be fully informed and have no nagging doubts about the truth of the matter.

■ Those who are searching for truth and meaning in their lives and may be tempted to join an organization that claims it has the truth that will lead to everlasting life, would do well to read this review written by someone who has been there and left.

■ Those who have left the movement and are having difficulty coming to terms with life outside the organization or adjusting to living without the constant guidance given by their Society will find this book of help.

■ Those who have left because of doubts about the Society and its teachings will find this documented history of the organization along with the examination of its key doctrines, fascinating reading.

■ Those still involved who are having difficulty making it all add up should find the courage to read an independent viewpoint.

■ Those who have friends or relatives they would like to reach out to or understand better, will gain a valuable insight into the workings of a Witness mind and the Society he or she belongs to.

This examination seeks to find whether Jehovah's Witnesses' claim to alone have "the truth" is valid. Some chapters are easier reading than others, but you will benefit most if you start at the beginning and read all the chapters in order. The chapters dealing with scripture contain suggestions as to how they apply. My opinions are only intended to encourage you in your search for truth. Any opinions you form must be based on your own research.

Throughout this book the Watchtower Society is measured against the Bible, as this is the holy book that they and other Christian sects use as their benchmark. It has to be remembered that although Judaeo-Christianity is one of the world's main religions, it is also the newest. Eastern approaches to the pursuit of truth predate Christianity by many thousands of years. A true seeker of truth would find their search incomplete if they were to exclude other such sincere worshipers without an examination of their beliefs. All religions contain an element of truth but can any one religion claim to contain all truth and exclude all others? That is a question that you would be unwise to allow someone else to answer on your behalf.

Thoughtful disagreement is essential to progress. As we learn, we grow and change. I have not attempted to offer an alternative, but to show that belief in God need not include living in fear of death at Armageddon when one's best fails to meet the requirements of the Watchtower Society. We should be free of such fear and pressure to pursue truth with open minds.

✳ ✳ ✳

If my writings help to promote such freedom and assist you in your search for truth, then my years spent as a Jehovah's Witness will not have been wasted.

TREVOR WILLIS

1

THE KNOCK ON YOUR DOOR

The First Call
"No thank you – I'm not interested!"

This is the most common response given to Jehovah's Witnesses as they call from door to door looking for converts. Your response may well have been the same. Perhaps like many people you already have a religion or beliefs that suit you. Then again you may have no time for religion or think that the idea of a god existing is naive. You may believe that you could never be drawn into their religion. The idea that you could become a fully involved Jehovah's Witness in a few years time may seem laughable at present.

Why do Jehovah's Witnesses continue such an intense cold calling campaign, in spite of the stony reception they receive?

It is because they are successful due to their training in overcoming negative responses. A survey carried out by sociologist James A. Beckford showed that 46% of all Witnesses are converted by this means. Only 3% seek out the movement on their own initiative. Many of the remainder have been raised in the religion.

The majority of people give no thought to Jehovah's Witnesses until they are confronted at their door. It is the element of surprise that gives the Witness an advantage. They are trained and prepared for the encounter; in most cases those they call on are not. An active Witness is one that calls from house to house and reports the time spent doing this. The most recent annual total of time spent in this activity and reported was over one billion hours. Their literature is produced in 137 languages. There are now approaching 6,000,000 active Jehovah's Witnesses in over 204 countries around the world. The semi monthly *The Watchtower* magazine has achieved a current print run of over 22,000,000 per issue.

Many of the people who joined last year did not have any intention of becoming involved until they were called upon. It is often due to lack of preparation and knowledge of Jehovah's Witnesses that people are caught off guard and become involved.

Whereas most people have heard of Jehovah's Witnesses, very few have a sound idea of their beliefs or the type of lives they are required to live. Along with yourself, your friends, relatives and neighbours are called on every two months on average. Unless you have a definite reason for not listening to their message it is inevitable that over a period of time, constant exposure to such an approach combined with the offer of literature, will result in you listening to their appeal. Perversely it is those who feel they could never be converted who are most vulnerable to persuasion.

The Attraction

The desire to worship or please God is only one of the many reasons why people involve themselves with Jehovah's Witnesses. We all have certain needs, which must be met in order for our lives to be fulfilled. For life to have meaning we must have a purpose. We set ourselves goals intellectually, spiritually, physically and emotionally. When we find ourselves lacking in stimulation in these areas we can suffer from depression.

To be a Jehovah's Witness means more than just belonging to a religion, it is a whole way of life and a community within itself. It can offer friendship, security and purpose. It can appeal to those who are looking for reassurance and guidance in their lives. It claims to have an answer for every question you could ask; questions about the past, the future, what is good or bad, right or wrong. It can give meaning to living in a world, which at times seems to have gone astray.

It is not only religious people who become involved, in fact their resistance can often be greater than those who profess no faith. As towns get larger and more impersonal, there lingers in many people a desire to belong to a close-knit village type of community to which they can contribute their personality. The need to belong and to feel needed is very human. To some, leading others and being looked up to is also important.

Jehovah's Witnesses, led by the Watchtower Society, initially appear to offer the security that is so missed in modern society today. To live among people who share the same purpose, goals and prejudices and share the same idea of what is right and wrong can be an attractive proposition.

To the average working man or woman looking for answers or direction in life or an elderly person who has little to look forward to, the offer of a helping hand by a friendly person offering to explain the purpose of life can be the first step to involvement with an organization which could alter their entire life.

The middle-aged lady with a pleasant smile who calls to chat about the problems of old age or the smartly dressed young man concerned about world conditions are trained representatives of the Watchtower Society. Their aim is to start you on the first rung of a ladder that is promised to lead to eternity. It is a ladder you should examine carefully as you could be trying to climb it for the rest of your life.

Jehovah's Witnesses have specialised in such an approach for over one hundred years. Most people would be unaware of their existence were it not for that "knock on your door."

Contagious Enthusiasm

The knock on your door is known as "the first call work." The persistence of the Witnesses is due to their belief in the imminent end of the present world system. They call for three reasons.

■   They believe they have been commissioned by God and would fail in their service to Him if they neglected to warn you.

■   Ultimately they would like you to join their organization because they see this step as the only way to salvation.

3

- Failing this they have a warning work to do. The warning is that all who fail to seek refuge in their Society will perish at Armageddon.

Calling from door to door is not easy. To some members it is the greatest test of their faith. Most Witnesses are extremely busy. They have to put their own interests in second place to find the time to call. Many go from door to door in a mechanical way so they can report the required amount of time and prove they are in "the truth." However some Witnesses genuinely care for the people they call on.

When I was a Witness I honestly believed that the only chance those I called on had of escaping death, when God brought an end to the world, as we know it; lay in my hands. Like many others, I forced myself on in the heat of summer and the cold of winter, often continuing for eight hours in the wind and rain.

I was just fifteen when I agreed to spend a minimum of 100 hours per month in this unpaid activity. The other days were for earning a living. Calling on so many people, some of whom were abusive, took a great deal of courage. Doors were regularly slammed in my face. I have been sworn at, shouted at, pushed, threatened, bitten by dogs, frog- marched down paths, laughed at, reported to the police and had my literature torn up.

Like those who still call from house to house, I did not believe I carried out this ministry in my own strength. Before going out I, along with others, asked God for his help to carry out his work. Witnesses still do this before calling. Looking back at the implications of the message I carried to the families I called on, the great majority of them were polite and showed great restraint, often expressing empathy for me and what I was trying to do.

I share these memories with you because it is important to realize how deeply involved many of the Jehovah's Witnesses who call on you are. It has been said that the greatest quality a salesman can possess is belief in his product – sincerity and enthusiasm follow naturally and are hard to resist, they are contagious. The Witnesses believe that they have been commissioned by God and take their authority from the Bible, believing they are following the example set by Jesus. The following quote is taken from their own *Watchtower* magazine and is addressed to non-Witnesses under the heading, "Why you should be interested" :

> When the son of God, Jesus Christ was on earth, he sent out his followers to announce the good news about God's heavenly Government. In fact, he instructed his disciples in the manner in which they should present this unusual and important message at each home and what steps to take where householders fail to show genuine interest. Show interest – It means your life!

> It is of interest to note that Jesus Christ compared the responses of our day to those days of Noah and of Sodom and Gomorrah … He indicated that many would not respond to the message of good news of God's Kingdom but would be preoccupied with the everyday affairs of life and thus show no interest in what Jehovah purposes to do. The message is one of life-or-death importance. Failure to listen would be costly. To take no note or show any interest is a serious sin … To rouse the attention of those to whom he spoke he admonished: "Pay attention to how you listen." "Let him that has ears listen." "Listen to me, all of you, and get the meaning." "Listen and get the sense of it."

> Therefore the next time a Jehovah's Witness calls at your home, it will be of your benefit to say: "Come in, I am interested."
>
> *THE WATCHTOWER* – 1 FEBRUARY 1988 – PAGE 29

Provoking Response

After a friendly introduction the Witness will start to form an opinion about your potential as a possible "sheep-like one." This is a term for someone with the correct disposition to become a Jehovah's Witnesses. Should they be unable to gain ground with you, they will usually conclude their visit by pointing out the dangers you face if you remain outside of the safety of their organization.

To remain in this state means you are a "goat-like one." The Witness will feel the visit has served a purpose and not been a total waste if he has sounded the warning. Before resorting to this the Witness will try to appeal to your desire to live in a better world.

To some, the promise of an end to loneliness, worry, poverty, sickness and the many other problems than can enter our lives, can be tempting. Those who have suffered a bereavement or reversal of circumstances are particularly susceptible to such an approach. The offer of a loved one who has died returning very soon to live with them on earth forever, can be irresistible. When I went from door to door I was trained to vary my approach according to the person I was calling on.

- I would ask a mother if she worried what the world would be like for her children when they grew up. Would she like them to live in a better world?

- To someone elderly or unwell I would ask if they were aware of the Bible's promise that within the next few years sickness and death would be no more.

- If, say a man, had no time for religion I would ask if he felt that the churches had let people down. I would tell him that religion was responsible for some of the worst wars ever fought.

- To someone who was obviously annoyed at my visit, I would ask if he or she wondered why we kept calling when most people considered us a nuisance.

- Current events were always taken into account. If the news focused on disaster, I would enquire whether they believed God should prevent such suffering. Or perhaps such events had caused them to believe that there is no God. Any recent news could be referred to – corruption in politics, a church leader in disgrace, public disorder, pollution and damage to our environment, social problems caused by the type of society we live in.

The list is almost endless. I could usually touch the right nerve and draw the householder into a discussion. People love to complain, to say more should be done about the problems in the world. Most people have a favourite hobbyhorse. There is almost no subject that cannot be used to convince a talkative person that they are right to feel unhappy with their lot in life or the world in general.

Do you feel it is unfair the way unpleasant people seem to get on well in life while decent people seem to take second place? You may agree with this sentiment or believe it to be a negative generalisation – either way it is likely that you would respond to such a question. Response is what that Witness is looking for. Anger, sarcasm and criticism are all expected reactions.

I called on a number of members of another small religious group who were concentrated in the area I lived in, who had been advised on how to deal with Witnesses. They would stand and quietly listen, looking attentive but not speaking. They would not answer questions, look away or shut the door, but just stand and wait until I left, hard to do and impolite, but very effective.

The idea is to make you respond! If you do choose to discuss with a Witness, insist that they answer your questions. I do mean answer your questions to your satisfaction, not use them as a route back to the point they came to make.

There are a number of pertinent questions that can be asked, but I have avoided listing them here, as it is my hope that the information in the following chapters will help you to form your own ideas. Further to this, your approach will depend very much on whether you hold with Christian teachings or are of another persuasion.

Jehovah's Witnesses are not confidence tricksters. The membership is, on the whole, sincere and devoted. The hope they encourage others to embrace is a hope they have built their lives around.

The Call that Changed my Life

From among many hundreds of examples, I have selected a few brief real-life quotes to illustrate how that knock on the door has changed the lives of many people :

As the years went by, I could still see the hypocrisy of and emptiness of life, as a general rule, in so many traditional churches, as they were then. Finally I left and for a period there was just the

Bible and me and then the Watchtower at the door! Wonderful! They had all the answers! Joy! I loved it! I was happy! I loved Jehovah God. I felt close to him, I understood all his plans for us. I loved my dear friends. More friends than I had ever had before. Wonderful friends. Mrs W.B.

About ten years ago I was spiritually at my lowest ebb, an extremely dangerous condition to be in if a Witness should knock at your door – and one did just that, on a snowy January afternoon. That call was to change my life! Apart from my spiritual void, the time of year was against me too. Who feels their brightest on a winter's day, particularly when one has been alone since Christmas breakfast time?

I was just thinking about making myself a cup of tea and settling down with a book, when the knock came. When I opened the door I was confronted by a small muffled little figure sprinkled with snow ... she looked so cold I asked her in for a cup of tea. I told her I was a Catholic and did not want to talk about her faith, and that I had only asked her in because of the weather not to talk religion ... In the end of course, I told her how I felt about the Church and of the numerous questions I had that never seemed to be answered to my satisfaction. "I'll answer them," she said, "from God's word, the Bible," And she did! I was completely taken aback. Here was an ordinary soul, a housewife like myself who answered questions that priests did not seem able to. Mrs J.F.

I was living happily with my wife and 5 children, we went to one of Christendom's churches, Episcopal. One day a Witness couple came preaching at our door. They had such a good line that my wife fell for it. I guess I did too. Mr C.P.

I had become a born-again Christian in 1979 when I was a senior in high school. I was really involved in the Baptist Church, and then I got married. My husband was born-again also but wasn't really dedicated even though he knew he should be. We attended church quite often but our spiritual life just seemed to slow down. The Witnesses came to my door little more than a year ago. I was puzzled by a lot of their doctrines, especially with Jesus being an angel. But their dedication really attracted me;

and they always seemed to be able to answer my questions, backing it up with the Bible.   Mrs S.R.

Mine is a typical story, I was a child of the 60's; my friends went to Vietnam, and I became a rock star. Band fell apart due to drugs and I searched for answers. Those answers came with blue eyes, blonde hair and a 'Truth Book' in her hands. (I am referring, of course, to *The Truth That Leads To Eternal Life*, published by The Watchtower Bible & Tract Society)   Mr D.H.

Once upon a time there was a very foolish young woman, namely me. One day I heard a knock at my door and guess what was there? You guessed it – Jehovah's Witnesses, and being the foolish young woman I was I let them in. They told me that the end of the world was coming very soon and that God would destroy me at Armageddon if I didn't become one of Jehovah's Witnesses, and not only me but my blond-haired, blue-eyed, pretty little girl I held on my hip, Lauren.

You have to realize that I was terrified as they showed me scripture after scripture that seemed to bear out what they were saying, I loved my little girl and didn't want anything to happen to her and surely I didn't want her killed by a vengeful God because of me … Soon I was baptised as one of Jehovah's Witnesses because they were God's people. Well, soon after I joined they told me that Armageddon was coming in 1975 and it was necessary for me to work hard going from door to door selling the literature and conducting home 'Bible Studies' in order to save myself and my little girl.   Mrs G.N.

Door to Door

The door-to-door calling is not a haphazard affair. A map of each congregation area is taken out and cut into pieces, each covering a few roads. These are then stuck on cards and filed.

The territory is then covered in a systematic way ensuring regular and even "witnessing" as the cards are dated and rotated. All householders who are out are noted. These are called on again before the map portion is returned. All hours worked and all return visits made are recorded, along with literature that is accepted. Each member makes a monthly report on a special

9

form. These are totalled and the congregation's average noted. These will form the basis of goals to set for the congregation, also to give an indication of which areas need attention. A separate annual record card is kept for each **publisher** – the term given to those who report their time. Reporting time is a requirement for baptism. If a publisher shows poor averages or fails to report for a while, they are visited to find out the reason.

Most Witnesses assume this is a system worked out by the Society. Those in the business of direct selling will be all too familiar with this method of organized cold canvassing.

Many householders believe that accepting a piece of literature at their door will get rid of the Witness – the exact opposite is true. Should you show interest or accept literature, a return call will be made. The Witness will follow a theme previously used that seemed to capture your interest. Your comments and personal details are recorded on another form. These are analysed to decide the best way to approach you on the return visit.

The idea is to get you to agree to spend one hour each week in your own home studying a Watchtower Society book, which the Witness has decided will suit you best. It is hoped that this will lead to your accepting invitations to larger study groups or visiting the Kingdom Hall where the congregation meets.

2

INSIDE THE CONGREGATION

Meetings

Once fully involved you would be expected to attend two evening meetings, one lasting an hour and the other two hours, also a two-hour Sunday meeting. You would be expected to spend some hours each week preparing for these meetings. The Kingdom Halls are set out in a similar way to school assembly halls. They are quite unlike any Church meeting you may have attended.

Preparing for and attending these meetings takes considerable time, particularly if you are male and progress to taking a lead from the platform. Often other interests have to be sacrificed and this is encouraged and expected. Attendance at these meetings comes before everything else. Members often alter their employment to ensure they can attend all meetings. In all my years at home no member of my family ever missed a meeting unless ill. There was no excuse for missing a meeting.

The meetings are comprised of question and answer discussions, lectures and audience training in public speaking. The main purpose of all meetings is to train and encourage members to spend several more hours a week calling on others to return the favour they received when they were called upon.

The main source of instruction to the members comes from *The Watchtower* magazine, particularly the question and answer articles designed for the main Sunday meeting. The information in these articles is believed to reflect God's thoughts to the members as revealed through the Society.

These articles never state who wrote them. They are just accepted as spiritual food passed on by those at the very top of the organization. Over the many years that this policy has been in force, an aura of great mystery has built up and adds to the feeling of powerful invincibility that the Society enjoy. This anonymity helps to support the belief that God himself is communicating through the Watchtower. Due to this, no blame can ever be attributed to an individual for failed prophecies or changes in beliefs.

All main meetings begin and end with a "kingdom song." These songs are taken from the Society's own songbook. All church hymnbooks are completely banned and even the word hymn is never used. Such hymnbooks are said to contain false teachings and be used by churches that are part of the Devil's organization. The words in the Watchtower songbook are designed to highlight the beliefs of the Witnesses.

As time progressed you would be expected to participate in these meetings. Initially by answering from your seat and then by joining others on the platform. You would also be expected to take a share in the cleaning, upkeep and repair of the Kingdom Hall. In addition, you would be encouraged to contribute financially.

As you became involved you would be shown the need to end all friendships with non-Witnesses. This is seen as an essential step on the road to conversion as most of the friends you have will be against you becoming a Witness. By ending all old friendships you would find yourself in a completely new environment. All members refer to each other as brother or sister, a term reserved for those who have accepted the teachings of the Watchtower Society and are regularly attending meetings. Once you have made a break with all previous social ties with the world outside the Watchtower Society, the next step is inevitable.

Will You Join the Dance?

During this gradual progression of involvement you would be

brought to the realization that your salvation depends upon water baptism. This shows your total dedication to carrying out God's will as relayed to you by the Watchtower Society.

Before being allowed to take this step you would be required to answer a number of questions designed to make sure that you are totally in harmony with the organization's view of all matters relating to every aspect of your beliefs and lifestyle.

Before I was baptised I had to answer questions such as:

- Why should you be willing to preach the good news to all kinds of people in your territory?

- Why should you take most seriously your responsibility to share the good news with others?

- Whose teaching and instruction is given at congregation meetings?

- In addition to any material contributions to advance the good news, what should we offer that is even more important?

- What pattern set in ancient Israel serves as a model for giving material support to the Kingdom work today?"

The questions selected above relate to what is expected of baptism candidates rather than those relating to the beliefs that must be accepted. In all there were 122 questions that had to be answered correctly. They are shown in full in the book *Organized to Accomplish Our Ministry*. Should any answers fail to meet with approval, the candidate had to agree to further study and apply at a later date when he or she could try again. Assigned elders made the final decision as to whether he or she could be baptised.

To the candidates, this ritual takes on great meaning, as it is only by water baptism that they can be accepted into the organization. Until this takes place they cannot hope to be spared from the destruction at Armageddon, which could come any day, as it is already overdue by more than a hundred years; that is a hundred years from the first date given by the Society for this event, as you will see later.

Baptism

I was just thirteen years old when I qualified for baptism. It seems very young looking back, but at the time I was aware that to be fully accepted and to be sure of surviving Armageddon, it was a step I had to make. Failing this I would have had to rely on my parent's baptism to count for me. Baptism only takes place at the twice-yearly assemblies. The candidates for baptism sit at the front of the audience and listen to a short lecture, and are then asked to stand and collectively answer two questions, which are read out loud to them. Prayer is then offered and they then depart to the baptism pool. Sometimes this is in the same venue, in which case the whole audience of perhaps a thousand people will witness this event. Should it be an international assembly in a sports stadium then many tens of thousands will watch.

In my own case, the baptism, which was a happy occasion, took place in a specially constructed small baptism pool built into the floor of one of the Kingdom Halls near where the assembly was taking place. The water was warm and the people present were kind and happy for me. The event brought great joy to the brothers and sisters who knew me. I was warmly congratulated and experienced a feeling of well-being and deep satisfaction that I was pleasing those I loved and dedicating my life to serve God.

It is interesting to note the change that has taken place in the vows taken just prior to to baptism. The two questions that I was expected to give an affirmative to are shown here :

■ Have you repented of your sins and turned around, recognising yourself before Jehovah God as a condemned sinner who needs salvation, and have you acknowledged to him that this salvation proceeds from him, the Father, **through his son Jesus Christ?**

■ On the basis of this faith in God and his provision for salvation, have you dedicated yourself unreservedly to do his will henceforth as he reveals it to you **through Jesus Christ and through the Bible under the enlightening holy spirit?**

These questions, or vows, were changed in 1985 to the following :

■ On the basis of the sacrifice of Jesus Christ, have you repented of your sins and dedicated yourself to Jehovah to do his will?

■ **Do you understand that your dedication and baptism identify you as one of Jehovah's Witnesses, in association with God's spirit-directed organization?** Having answered yes to these questions, candidates are in the right heart condition to undergo Christian baptism.

The above changes are rather significant. The lines that I have highlighted change the basis of the dedication. The new vows bind the candidate to the Watchtower Society. Also there is no longer any mention of the revealing of God's will through Jesus Christ or the Bible by means of Holy Spirit.

There is a legal significance to this. Should a member who has been excommunicated for apostasy try to sue the Society on the basis that their vows were to serve God through Jesus Christ and claim that they are still doing this, the Society could respond by saying that their vows specified that they remain a Witness, under the direction of the Society.

This further illustrates the way that the Watchtower Society has slowly moved itself into the position that many other Christians have reserved for Jesus.

Having been baptised, I was now expected to earn my salvation, in order to be saved, paying by instalments. If I failed at any point, or disagreed with any new teachings the Society introduced, I thought I would lose all the credit I had built up and either lose my salvation or knuckle down and start again.

The Society's publication *Babylon the Great has Fallen* (1963) explains :

> The person now righteous in God's sight should keep on prac-
> tising righteousness. The one who is holy as a slave of God
> should continue being made holy. Otherwise they will lose all
> the credit they have built up by their previous righteousness
> and holiness. But if they keep on in righteousness and holiness,
> they will at last have an accumulated credit with God and be
> richly rewarded for this. What a warning and an encouragement!
>
> PAGE 672

15

This is in contrast to the Bible passages shown below :

> For all have sinned and fall short of the glory of God,
> and it is as a free gift that they are being declared
> righteous by his undeserved kindness through the
> release by the ransom (paid) by Jesus Christ.
>
> (Romans 3: 22-24 –
> **THE NEW WORLD TRANSLATION –**
> **the Society's own Bible –**
> **from now on referred to as NWT**)

> For it is by his grace you are saved, through trusting
> in him; it is not your own doing. It is God's gift,
> not a reward for work done.
>
> (Ephesians 2:8 –
> **THE NEW ENGLISH BIBLE –**
> **from now on referred to as NE**)

The Bible indicates that there is a standard for Christians but states that being declared righteous is a free gift and not the result of accumulated credit. Nevertheless a trained Witness may persuade you otherwise and encourage you to join and earn your salvation.

Obedience

Should you be accepted into the movement you would be expected to follow without question the dictates of the Watchtower Society under the threat of the world's imminent end. You would be told that you are personally responsible for every life lost at Armageddon if you could have done more to warn people but failed to do so. The penalty required will be your life. Any difficulty or opposition should be blamed on direct interference by the Devil :

> Infuriated by his debased condition and knowing that his time
> is short Satan, with his demons, makes every effort to interfere
> with the preaching work of Jehovah's people. This brings

16

Jehovah's servants into the battle lines of spiritual warfare ... If we are to come off victorious on Jehovah's side, we must not let up in the fight but keep our spiritual armour in tact and push ahead in the all out war against every wicked machination of the Devil.   ORGANIZED TO ACCOMPLISH OUR MINISTRY PAGE 163

Christians believe that there is a Devil who is opposed to their belief in Christ, but do not claim that every religion in the world is in league with him, engaged in a campaign to overthrow the Watchtower Society.

To be a Jehovah's Witness you would be expected to condemn all other religions and believe them to be part of an organization run by the Devil. To such an extent, that should a relative marry, you would not be allowed to take part in the church service. Churches are considered part of Satan's organization which is in direct opposition to God's – namely their own.

It has been said that the Christian Church is an organism not an organization. All sects with their different characteristics and cultures make up one church. The unifying factor is their belief in Jesus Christ.

The Witnesses do not claim to be a part of the worldwide Christian Church. They are totally opposed, considering their small sect to be the only acceptable group to worship with. Their Society has always claimed to be the only true church. Recently they have tried to claim that orthodox Christianity, despite its size, is in fact a sect. They themselves cannot be considered a sect, as they are a continuation of the original Christian movement.

As a Witness you would never be able to integrate with the many Christians from other denominations, enter their churches or share a service with them. Despite your refusal to tolerate the religion of others you would be expected to persuade others to accept your religion, actively encouraging them to come to your church.

Running Ahead

If a member believes any teaching of the Society to be false, they must not tell anyone. The Society states that if it is wrong, then

17

it will in its own time alter the false beliefs – officially. To try to hasten this process or expose the false teaching is termed "running ahead", at worst, apostasy. All beliefs are referred to as "truths" until they are changed and then they become "old truths" but are never referred to as falsehoods or lies.

To run ahead of the Society is a sin in their eyes. Members must remain silent and pretend they agree with all official teachings. This includes encouraging those they call on in their ministry to accept the false teaching. Distributing Watchtowers that carry known errors is also part of their ministry. If the Society does eventually alter its mind on the matter, then the members are allowed to alter theirs. If the Society never does or comes up with a third alternative, the members must follow suit. It claims to be responsible for the personal beliefs of the membership.

> We should meekly go along with the Lord's theocratic organization and wait for further clarification, rather than baulk at the first mention of a thought unpalatable to us and proceed to quibble and mouth our criticisms and opinions as though they were worth more than the slave's provision of spiritual food. Theocratic ones will appreciate the Lord's visible organization and not be so foolish as to pit against Jehovah's channel their own human reasoning and sentiment and personal feelings.
>
> THE WATCHTOWER – 2 JANUARY 1952 – PAGE 8

All members are expected to conform to a strict code of conduct and morality. Sex outside marriage is an offence, which usually results in the offender being excommunicated. For a first offence leniency is sometimes shown if the member appears to be truly repentant. Homosexuality is strictly banned. Their stance on these and other matters of conduct are supported by quoting from the Bible :

> Make no mistake: no fornicator or idolater, none who are guilty either of adultery or of homosexual perversion, no thieves or grabbers or drunkards or slanderers or swindlers, will possess the Kingdom of God.   1 CORINTHIANS 5:9,10 – NE

Will You Walk a Little Faster?

Once involved in the congregation the initial attention shown to you would begin to wane. You would be expected to attend all the meetings, make regular comments from your seat and share in the door-to-door work. This is in addition to other communal activities.

Articles in *The Watchtower* along with regular lectures encourage the members to mix only with those who are "strong in the truth" or "close to the organization." The idea being that if members become weary then they are not showing enough faith. In order to enjoy continued acceptance they must keep running. When the pressure becomes hard to bear they are reminded of the scripture :

> Boys will without fail tire out and grow weary, and young men themselves will without fail stumble, but those who are hoping in Jehovah will regain power. They will mount up with wings like eagles. They will run and not grow weary; they will walk and not tire out. ISAIAH 40:30,31 – NWT

So there is no excuse for slowing down, this would be taken as an admission of "spiritual weakness." Those who show such a tendency will at first be encouraged or "strengthened." If they do not respond sufficiently other members will slight them, withdrawing their warmth. They find that invitations to tea and other social functions are not forthcoming. If they try to remedy this situation by inviting members to their home, excuses will be made. The danger of accepting an invitation from a member who has been labelled "spiritually weak" is that they themselves will in time be blacklisted.

Clearly with such a rigorous program of indoctrination it is wise to have all the facts about the beliefs of the Witnesses and make certain that you are in full agreement with their methods before allowing yourself to be persuaded onto the treadmill. Being a Witness leaves little time for other pursuits. This is the idea. Once involved, the "New World Society," as their organization is sometimes termed, becomes your whole world.

A Woman's Place

Women in the congregation do not share the same status as men. They are not allowed to lecture from the platform or make any announcement directly to the audience. When they are allowed on the platform, they must address another woman while the audience listens in and only if a man remains on the platform. They cannot offer prayer on behalf of the congregation or even say grace out loud over a meal in the presence of a baptised male. They may offer prayer in the presence of a male who has not been baptised but must cover their heads to do this.

They cannot be appointed as elders or even to the lower rank of ministerial servant. This excludes them from having any say in who qualifies for baptism or who is to be disfellowshipped. The exclusive male-run leadership claim their authority to exclude women in this way is taken from the Bible. (1 Corinthians 1:1-16, 1 Corinthians 14: 31-35, Ephesians 5:22,23, 1 Timothy 2:12)

This idea of male headship is taken to extremes among Witnesses. The women members, or sisters, are not allowed to be in charge of the supply of literature to other members at Kingdom Hall meetings or give out the canvassing territory maps. Even borrowing books from a hall library, must be overseen by a male member. They are not allowed to deal with congregation accounts, decisions on decorating, or the running of any department. They are allowed to be actively involved in weekly hall cleaning, though again this must be organized by a male. It is difficult to see how the principle of male headship in spiritual matters can be used to exclude women members from having any official authority or influence in the congregation, even in matters that are entirely secular.

Some women resent being suppressed in this way, but manage to gain considerable influence working through their husbands – but then this is not unique to their Society. The positive side of this exclusion is that the female members are under considerably less pressure than their male counterparts, as they are not expected to reach out for appointments or develop their skills as lecturers and many are quite content with the present arrangement.

Assemblies

In addition to the activities already outlined you would be expected to attend a circuit assembly every six months. This involves spending a day at a chosen venue large enough to seat upwards of a thousand people. This is a larger version of the other meetings. When I was involved, these assemblies lasted for three days. This gave us the opportunity to take part in a massive canvassing effort in the surrounding area. In many areas, as the Witnesses have become more prosperous, they have acquired their own venues such as converted cinemas, which are used every weekend by members from a larger area. Due to this, the surrounding areas are no longer canvassed.

Annually a series of gatherings of gigantic proportions take place around the world in various stadiums. These rallies give members a further chance to demonstrate their devotion, not just by attending, but also by helping to set up the event. Many members have spent months working to prepare the catering and literature sales departments, on a totally voluntary basis, some giving up their jobs to be available. Recently, in countries affected by the stricter European food laws, the vast and impressive catering effort has had to be curtailed, which has reduced the amount of volunteer labour required.

When these assemblies take place they last the best part of a week and provide an impressive show of strength for the Society. The impeccable behaviour and tidiness at these events has drawn much favourable comment from outsiders who have attended and demonstrate the high degree of discipline that Jehovah's Witnesses have developed.

Reaching Out

Once involved, the greatest pressure is placed on male members. They are expected to progress through the ranks until they are appointed as **elders**. All male members are expected to desire this position and the striving to attain an appointment is known as "reaching out." This appointment involves much responsibility and only those who have successfully trained as public speakers can hold such an office. This ability will then

21

be used to the full. Those who assist the elders are known as **ministerial servants.**

Those who show the right aptitude, which mostly consists of unquestioning obedience to the Society, can progress to positions of even higher authority and may even be invited to serve at a Bethel Home. The organization is masterminded from these Homes, which are basically printing plants. To receive such an invitation is a great honour. Such a person is thought to have been approved by the officials of God's organization and therefore God himself. Such a person would be taken into the confidence of the top officials.

Such trust has to be earned and this can be achieved by taking the next step on the ladder by becoming a **pioneer**. A pioneer is a male or female who spends one thousand hours per year going from door to door and conducting Bible studies. For many years the requirement was twelve hundred hours per year. A "vacation pioneer," now known as "temporary pioneer," is one who agrees to spend a proportionate amount time in this activity for just one month.

3

BUYING OUT
THE TIME

Life at School

As a schoolboy I lived a double life. In the evening I would go from door to door with my father or attend a meeting. Sometimes I would address an audience of one hundred or more adults from the platform. I would rub shoulders with men and women many times my age. They were kind and complimentary towards me, praising my comments or telling me what a fine "talk" I had given, being a lecture from the platform.

This was my world! These were the people I was soon to live with in a paradise earth, when my school and teachers had been destroyed. In the morning I would return to school. My classmates knew nothing of my other life. My teachers would sometimes cane me for failing to do my homework. I accepted this as a necessary persecution I must bear in order to pre-study for and attend the meetings. It was a matter of priority.

My day at school would begin with sitting alone in a classroom while the rest of the school attended assembly. I was forbidden to worship with them, so I would sit and pray or recall the events of the night before. I was not allowed to join the school orchestra or take part in the annual school play. I never belonged to a school sports team or took part in any team event that might mean spending a moment more than was absolutely necessary at my "worldly school." Weekends away canoeing and camping were also taboo. To be a "boy scout" was totally banned.

Children of the Witnesses are forbidden access to many of the self-esteem enhancing activities that are open to other children. They are brought up to believe that they are different and separate from the world. They do not fully integrate with their schoolmates or teachers, due to their resistance to being fully involved with the education process, and their training to avoid forming friendships with worldly people.

More so than other children, their main security comes from winning the approval of their parents. They find that to win this approval they must do whatever the Society and their parents tell them will win Jehovah God's approval. I was told, by my own parents that if I ever left the religion they would never talk to me again. If I were to ever marry outside the religion the same penalty would apply. Although these threats are not always carried out, the Witness child grows up believing that the continuation of their whole world depends upon gaining their parents approval.

In addition to this pressure to conform, is the threat that God himself will kill the child, if he or she should go against their parent's wishes. The child is also puzzled by the parent's willingness to lose them in this way and often concludes that the parents do not love him or her. How can they threaten a child they love in this way, or say that the God they love may kill their child? As a child I concluded that I meant very little to my parents. Not all Witness parents act in this way. Those that do, say that they are practising a form of principled love for the child. Unfortunately children do not interpret threats of his kind as love. Nor as far as I know do most adults.

Attending school was a legal requirement. As long as I left school with sufficient training to go from door to door as a pioneer, the time spent there could be justified. I was repeatedly told that schoolmates were bad association. Time with them was to be kept to a minimum. They were not invited to my home and I was forbidden to go to theirs. I would turn down all invitations to birthday parties and other celebrations. Although I was sent cards I was never allowed to return the gesture.

Despite the restraint I showed towards my classmates they were friendly towards me, though disappointed that I avoided them, and made excuses for my anti-social behaviour. It hurt me to reject their friendship but even more to think that they were soon to be killed because their parents were not Jehovah's Witnesses. When they discussed their extra school activities or career plans I would look at the ground. Until the last possible moment I allowed them and my teachers to believe that I was staying on to take exams. To disclose my intentions would have meant me being placed in the lowest grade among the school's rougher element. A few weeks before I left school I explained that I was leaving school to pioneer and support myself by window cleaning.

The two years leading up to my leaving school seemed to last forever. I spent every holiday from the age of thirteen, vacation pioneering and mixing with the established pioneers in my congregation. They constantly encouraged me to leave school as soon as possible and join them in the life saving work. Those raised as strict Witnesses are trained to view the world around them in an abstract way. The real world is life within the Society. Life at school simply becomes a distraction.

At school I would gaze out of the window and think about my other life. My teachers told me that I was dreamer but could do well at any subject I chose, if only I would stop daydreaming and concentrate. How could they know that I had another life apart from school? I viewed school as a prison, which restrained me from joining the pioneers. The passing months were a diminishing sentence.

After leaving school I had no close contact with anyone outside the organization, even those in the congregation were vetted for suitability. If anyone did not fit the mould I would be discouraged from associating with him or her. This attitude toward association permeates the whole movement at all levels.

I clearly remember a young Italian "brother" who left school and embarked on a seven-year apprenticeship in engineering. Those in the pioneer service told me that this showed he did not love Jehovah God and was only interested in material things. They advised me to stay away from him as he was a bad influence and would discourage me from entering the pioneer service.

As I was forbidden to have any association with those outside the Society, I was desperately short of friends of my own age and felt reluctant to avoid my friend and "brother," so I told my parents what had been said. They told me this was good advice and that the father was also to blame as it was his wish the boy should receive secular training. With Armageddon so close, the idea of training to earn a living was wrong and showed a lack of faith. I was told to avoid the whole family, as they were all bad association.

The young man is now supporting a family and serving in the same congregation, thirty years after he was judged and condemned along with his family for assuming his social responsibility to train himself to meet the challenge of paying his way in the world. I feel regret that I did not follow my own feelings and show true friendship. The Society would give warnings in the form of Watchtower articles and continue to do so. Talking of some of the members they wrote :

> However because they have allowed themselves to be unduly affected by this system's philosophy and empty deception, they may remark: "Pioneering is not for everybody. Besides, in today's economy you need a university education if you are going to make it." Materialistic and fleshly reasoning are part and parcel of the elementary things of the world – the fundamental precepts and beliefs of worldlings! Yielding to it can cause irreparable spiritual damage.
>
> THE WATCHTOWER – 15 JULY 1985 (PAGE 13)

How could we possibly be friends with those who had chosen college or university over pioneering? They were almost "worldlings!" My teachers went to great lengths to encourage me to continue on at school. They tried to tell me that the Watchtower Society was misleading me. I had already been warned that the Devil would use my teachers to try and weaken my faith, so I refused to consider their advice. I was trained to ignore any comments that were unfavourable towards the Society; it was a matter of loyalty. I warned them that the end of the world system was months away and that their lives were in danger.

The Society has always tried to make young minds believe that it is the will of God himself that they abandon all ambition, or higher education, or a career, in favour of promoting their beliefs :

As you think about your future, no doubt questions run through your mind. Should I go to university and seek a career as a doctor, a lawyer, or a scientist? Does the dream of climbing the corporate ladder to financial success and recognition intrigue me? Would I become a famous name in the arts through acting or painting? Or, as a youth devoted to Jehovah God, should I choose the full-time ministry as my career ... ?

Youths how will you use your future? For yourself or fully for Jehovah? Prayerfully consider the goal of full-time service now in your youth. Imitate Jesus by living the rest of your life 'for God's will.' It will prove to be a protection from harmful worldly ambitions, careers and associations. Analyse your circumstances and set a specific date as your goal for entering full-time service. Work towards it. Pray for Jehovah's help to attain it.

THE WATCHTOWER – 15 APRIL 1986 – PAGES 28-30

A representative from the London head office came to our town when I was fifteen, the earliest age for leaving school at that time. I asked him whether I should stay on at school until I was sixteen so I could take my exams. He answered in this way :

Just think how the angel will view you when he comes at Armageddon to destroy those outside the organization and he sees you busy with your exams when you could be pioneering. You haven't time to waste – Armageddon could be here any day now.

I waited in fear to leave school and prove that I was no part of the worldly schooling system.

Pioneering

The pressure never ceases. Every hour of every day is expected to be spent in the Society's service. Members are told that the time they take back for secular work, or to attend to the essentials of living, or some occasional recreation, is loaned to them, as all time is God's – the Society's. All time is to be spent in furthering the movement. This makes it difficult to pursue any worthwhile commercial endeavour.

Despite expecting it's members to minimise secular interests and avoid higher education, the Watchtower Society themselves use modern technology to the full and have the most advanced printing presses in the world. Those who run these printing plants are trained to the highest standard. The Society's real estate acquisition programme is phenomenal.

The aim of every convert should be to attain the status of pioneer. This is open to both men and women. The 1,000 hours per year they spend in door-to-door activity is in addition to attending meetings and a personal study programme of Society literature. Parents were encouraged to put pressure on their children to make them pioneer even threatening to make them leave home if they did not conform :

An elder in Korea encouraged his four children to pioneer. At a circuit assembly he and the four children were interviewed. The oldest daughter related how she had been the highest scholastically in her high school. She herself wanted to go to college at one point. However, her father informed her that, while she was free to choose such a course, she could not expect financial support from him. She changed her mind about college, and now she is enjoying the many blessings as a pioneer.

The next oldest, a son, told how he also wanted to go to college and follow a worldly course. But his father sat down and reviewed the scriptures with him. His father also told him that, if he insisted on following a worldly course, he would also have to find another place to live. He heeded his father's counsel and is very grateful that his father was kind but firm in his stand. The two younger children explained that they were impressed by what had happened to the two older ones. From the beginning they planned to become pioneers. The youngest son gave up his high school education to pioneer.

THE KINGDOM MINISTRY – MAY 1973 – PAGE 6

I doubt if this controlling father explained to his four children, that he would not be financially supporting them for the rest of their lives whatever they did. He no doubt passed on the Society's assurances that there were only a few years at most remaining of the wicked system they lived in.

As a young man growing up in this environment, it was made clear to me that any one who could pioneer but chose not to, did not love Jehovah and would be cold- shouldered by their family. We were warned that our very lives would be in danger at Armageddon if we chose the worldly course of pursuing an education.

The pressure to conform was immense. Like many other school leavers, I worked only two days per week to provide the bare essentials, so as to free myself to enter the pioneer service. The fact that pioneer service was an unpaid activity did not concern me at the time. I had been trained to view it as a career.

I became a good pioneer. I was commended and became totally absorbed in warning people. I was told that if I continued to apply myself then one day I might be invited to live at a Bethel Branch or share one of the other opportunities open to pioneers. These include travel of varying degrees and sometimes a posting to a foreign country as a missionary. All grades above being a pioneer provide an allowance that pays for the bare essentials and frees one from seeking part time employment.

As young pioneers sacrifice their career prospects to pursue this unpaid assignment, you may ask if they ever think about what would become of them, should they want to settle down and raise a family. When I was a pioneer a popular slogan was, "It's time to be settling up not settling down." The Watchtower Society explain it this way :

> Of course there may be a tempting offer of higher education or going into some field of work that promises material rewards. However, Jehovah God holds out to you young folks many marvellous privileges in his organization. Which will you take up? In view of the short time left, a decision to pursue a career in this system of things is not only unwise but also extremely dangerous. On the other hand, a decision to take advantage of what God offers through his organization opens up excellent opportunities for advancement as well as a rich meaningful life that will never end. Reports are heard of brothers selling their homes and property and planning to finish out the rest of their days in this old system in the pioneer service. Certainly this is a fine way to spend the short time remaining before the wicked world's end. KINGDOM MINISTRY – JUNE 1969 – PAGE 3

Many boys and girls like myself entered the pioneer service. Older members sold their homes, moved into rented accommodation to live on the proceeds and devote their time to warning people. "The rest of their days in this old system" turned into years and they had to salvage what they could from the costly mistake. The hardest hit were those who reached retirement age, disappointed and unprepared.

Careers

To become a Jehovah's Witness one must totally change their outlook towards work. Work has to take second place. The idea of pursuing a long-term career or striving to establish oneself in a profession is totally discouraged at every opportunity. Secular work is seen as an unfortunate distraction from the ultimate goal of every member – the pioneer service. Members are encouraged to leave school as soon as possible; to take an untrained menial job and pioneer is highly praised. To plan for the future financially shows a lack of faith that the world's system is ending at any moment.

Many of the members spend a great deal of time helping to build assembly halls and labouring voluntarily on other long-term ambitious projects for the movement. This is never seen as a lack of faith in the same way. The reason why has always escaped me. Young Witnesses are trained to view employment as a means of earning sufficient money to finance their Kingdom activities. This often leads to a hand to mouth existence. The great joy and sense of achievement that can be experienced by those who become absorbed in meaningful employment is sacrificed as a result.

This is a deliberate policy on the part of the Society; they know that such work satisfaction and ambition leads people away from devoting time to their cause. This attitude towards further education, promotion, self-betterment and ambition, affects adults as well. With few exceptions, adults are also held back from developing their abilities and reaching their full potential. The effect this has on their family's standard of living is considerable.

The financial sacrifices are not the greatest loss. Intelligent people, when trapped in employment that offers no challenge or room for expression, can experience intense frustration. Young Witnesses seldom consider their career carefully, not realising that the decision they make early on will affect the rest of their lives. Those who encourage them to abandon their career prospects in favour of the pioneer service, do not take the responsibility when young people find themselves unable to find meaningful employment in later years. They are told that pioneering was their own idea and that no one actually said "The End" was almost here, despite publishing this message for more than a hundred years!

It is inconceivable to a Witness that they could honour their God by developing their talent and contributing to the success of other people through their work. They must view all secular work as a distraction from promoting the teachings of the Watchtower Society. They are told that a satisfying career is a temptation that the Devil uses to sidetrack them from faithful service. God cannot possibly approve of them using the few remaining years of this system to develop their God given gifts – there will be time for that in "the new world". This attitude is summed up by the following quotation. These are the words of a member who left a prestigious New York music school after he studied with Jehovah's Witnesses :

A career in music demands exclusive devotion. In this it competes with our creator and the doing of his will. Music can be almost like a disease …

Frankly, I've come to look upon musical institutions as modern-day temples of worship that require people to devote their entire lives to music. But that is making a god out of it, and surely does not have the creator's approval.

AWAKE! – 8 AUGUST 1985 – PAGE 17

If adults of obvious intelligence can be influenced to view their careers in this way, what hope is there for children growing up in this climate to form a balanced view of their place in the world?

Many of the elders have come into the movement as adults with established careers, and continue to work full time and enjoy "the good life" while urging others to pioneer. The

Watchtower Society does not pay salaries. Young people would be wise to calculate the cost as carefully as the Watchtower Society does, and not give away the years they should be using to train for the challenge of earning a living in work they will enjoy, not for just a few months or years, but for the rest of their lives.

Marriage and Children

The Watchtower Society has for many years discouraged its members from having families. They point out that more time can be spent in the door-to-door work without the distraction of children. They say it is unwise to have a family when the "Great Tribulation" leading to Armageddon is almost upon us, and it will be harder for those with babies and children.

Many members have remained single because of this. Others have married but been afraid to have children and have lived their entire lives in anticipation of "The End," and passed away childless.

The pressure to pioneer instead of marrying and raising a family reached its peak in the 1970's, and then faded. In more recent years it was thought by many that the Society had altered its attitudes. As some who had passed by the opportunity of family life felt they had been wrongly advised, it was thought that the Society would continue to lay low on this subject, and allow the members to think for them without interference.

Unfortunately the Society knows that single or childless people who have devoted their lives to furthering the interests of their organization are too valuable to lose. Frightening members into pursuing such a course in life has gained them many pioneers in the past – too many to let sentiment stop them using the same tactics again. Raising children is not the most reliable way of enlarging the organization and takes far too long. Full-time pioneers are by far the most effective way.

At the 1987 summer assemblies, the pressure to avoid parenthood, or better still marriage, began to be applied again at the stadiums around the world. Later, *The Watchtower* contained two articles, "Childbearing Among God's People" and "Responsible Childbearing in This Time of the End." Among the many pages of advice and direction they stated :

While Paul (the Apostle) forbade neither marriage nor child-bearing, he obviously felt duty bound to warn his fellow Christians that such could bring about problems and distractions that might hinder them in their service to Jehovah ... Obviously, rearing children in the time of the end would not always be a pure joy. It could bring heartbreak, disappointment, and even danger.

The articles do not point out that this is a personal decision but liken the time we are living in to Noah's time and say of Noah's sons :

Second, they doubtless felt disinclined to bring children into a world where the badness of man was abundant in the earth ...

Our present day is also likened to the years leading up to Jerusalem's destruction :

Jewish historian Josephus relates that during the siege of Jerusalem in 70 CE*, children snatched food from the mouths of their fathers and mothers took food from the mouths of their infant children. He recounts how a Jewish woman killed her suckling baby, roasted the body, and ate part of it. Bringing children into the Jewish world in the final years leading up to the execution of Jehovah's judgments against Jerusalem in 607 CE and 70 CE could hardly be termed responsible childbearing.

1ST MARCH 1988

Many Witnesses who have reached middle age unmarried, childless and uneducated are told that the choices they made were their own responsibility and that the Society have never tried to predict when the "Old World" will end or tell its members how to live.

Under Pressure

There is no such thing as an acceptable level of service within the organization. There is always pressure to do more. Members are told that they cannot stop moving forward, because however

*CE – Common Era – The Christian era, used by non-Christians.

much they do it will not be enough to earn their salvation, if there is any chance they could be doing more. There is an over-riding feeling of guilt and fear that permeates the whole move-ment, and a feeling of isolation from the real world around, which is going to be destroyed at any time.

This is bound to affect the mental balance of some members. A study of Jehovah's Witnesses in Western Australia showed that they are more likely to be admitted to a psychiatric hospital than non members; three times more likely to suffer from schiz-ophrenia; four times more likely to suffer from paranoid schizo-phrenia. The study carried out by John Spencer concluded that :

> The study does not shed light on the question of symptom or defence mechanism, but suggests that either the Jehovah's Witnesses sect tends to attract an excess of pre-psychotic indi-viduals who may then break down, or else being a Jehovah's Witness is in itself a stress which may precipitate a psychosis. Possibly both of these factors may operate together.

In my own experience some members have a tendency to develop illness, as this is the only acceptable reason for missing meetings or door-to-door activity. After many years of offering illness as an excuse, some come to believe they really are unwell.

Living in anticipation of such a frightening event as the Witnesses vision of Armageddon and longing for a better world – just around the corner – is a recipe for mental strain and frustra-tion. Coupled with this is the totally negative view a Witness develops towards the present world, believing it all to be a giant failure, too bad to be evolved into a better world. Rather the people of the world are beyond hope and the best thing that can be done with them is to destroy them all and start over again!

A proverb in the Witnesses own Bible explains :

> Expectation postponed
> is making the heart sick,
> but the thing that is desired
> is the tree of life.
>
> PROVERBS 13:12 – NWT

4

KEEPING SEPARATE FROM THE WORLD

Workmates

Whether one is brought up a Witness or converted, many years of conditioning and counselling bring all members to view others in a critical way. They show the same attitude towards their workmates as they train their children to show at school towards their classmates. The minimum amount of time is to be spent at work or at school. However decent and upright a work-mate may be, he or she is viewed as a bad association. To have a drink after work or a meal at the weekend with such a person is seen as a compromise.

The Witnesses see themselves as a nation apart – God's special possession. They feel that they risk contamination every time they share a social occasion with "worldly people." The other reason is time. They are instructed to spend their spare time pro-moting the Watchtower Society, which is seen as serving God. All community activity is avoided as it involves contact with outsiders and it also takes time. The only cause they support is the Watchtower Society, who claim that they support God's Kingdom.

Friends in the Congregation

This embargo on friends does not only apply outside the congregation. Very pointed talks are regularly given, backed by Watchtower articles, to warn members of the dangers from within. The threat of contamination from those outside is easily avoided, but the unwary can form friendships on the inside, which may weaken their faith.

The danger is weak members. A weak member is someone who claims to be a brother or sister but does not attend all the meetings and is not regular in field service, the official name for door-to-door work. Even those that keep up a good appearance may be viewed as bad association if they do not make all the right noises.

All members, even children, are expected to raise their hand and comment when questions are addressed to the congregation. The quality and frequency of comment is seen as an accurate gauge of one's "heart condition." It is very easy to tell if a member is in tune with the latest thinking by his comments. If a brother is disturbed or annoyed over something he will remain silent. If he does answer any discord will usually show. All the members watch one another closely and listen for any signs of rebellion or independence developing. If two families should get together for say, Sunday tea, then the conversation will revolve around things to do with the congregation or the Society. These are termed "spiritual matters."

However close one may be to fellow members they must remain on their guard. If one confides a doubt or grievance, the friend will see it as his duty to report the conversation. It is seen as a test of loyalty. Will the member be loyal to his friend and remain silent or be loyal to Jehovah, alias the Society? Reporting a friend is not seen as a betrayal but rather a display of deep principled love for the friend. Members are encouraged to report each other so the weak member can be identified by the elders and helped. This involves adjusting his or her thinking to be in line with the others.

Members who are not totally in line find that they are unable to make friends within the congregation. Even if they do keep up appearances and keep their thoughts to themselves, they still do not have close friends. For this reason some will develop friendships with outsiders who they can confide in without fear of being reported. Those who are still able to feel the respect and affection for outsiders that this requires have not totally resigned themselves to the Society. In time they become more dissatisfied with the set-up and spend less time in spiritual activities. This leads to them being labelled as weak members and costs them the opportunity of socialising with strong members. In time they usually become upset by the way they are avoided and kept on the fringe, and leave completely.

Comparisons have been drawn between the Watchtower Society and the society portrayed in George Orwell's book *1984*. The similarities are striking.

The Witnesses are fond of saying that they have not got a friend in the world, the world being those outside the Society. When members go through a difficult time for domestic or financial reasons, they will find that they do not have a friend in the world – literally. Members are not supposed to have anything more than minor problems. It is an embarrassment to the congregation to have members with serious problems. They are expected to be above the worries that affect worldly people, so when members most need help they often find themselves avoided.

The danger in coming forward and showing oneself to be a true friend, is the risk of being identified with the member who is seen as giving a bad witness. Most members will not want to be seen associating with those who are struggling. Some will believe that the member with problems has lost God's spirit.

Relatives

The rules regarding friends apply to relatives but are applied more leniently. Most Witnesses will see their relatives but avoid forming any deep bond or regular visiting habits, unless they too belong to the world of the Witnesses. When families traditionally spend Christmas together or celebrate a birthday, the Witness will decline to join them.

Some will not attend Church weddings, even the wedding of their own son or daughter. Those that do will not join in the service. This is puzzling because they recognise the marriage as legally binding in God's eyes. As they believe God has yoked the couple together and witnessed the marriage, why can they themselves not witness the event? The purpose of attending a wedding is to recognise the marriage as binding, not to indicate one's own religious preference. I personally knew an elder's daughter who was a Witness but was about to marry a non-Witness. The elder was told, by the other elders that if he went to the wedding he would not be an elder when he got back. He missed his own daughter's wedding but was happy to visit them in the years that followed. To be fair, it is not only the Witnesses who take this stance. Marriage between those of different faiths has been a cause of conflict since the earliest times.

Although most Witnesses do not refuse to see relatives who belong to other faiths, their attitude towards them can lead to them drifting apart. Such relatives are automatically viewed by the Witness as being on the side of the Devil, in opposition to God, as the world is divided into these two camps. This can be offensive to relatives, who are also aware that the related Witness expects them soon to be killed off by the God the Witnesses love. Under the circumstances Jehovah's Witnesses seldom see relatives outside the Society. Should Witnesses who are related to a large number of Witness families leave the movement, they risk losing the affection of all their relatives.

Normally a father will place great importance on his son. The father knows that one day he will pass away and all that he has worked for will pass to his son. The son is looked to as the one who will continue his family line. Within the Watchtower Society the son is not seen in the same way. The father who is a Witness has no need to perpetuate his family line. He believes he will live forever on earth. If the son shares his faith then they will live together forever. If the son leaves the organization, he will be killed at Armageddon, the day of judgement. In this case the father would expect to outlive his son and grandchildren.

Non-Witnesses are surprised how easily a father can turn his back on a son who leaves, but it becomes understandable when they realize that the father does not place the same importance on a son as a father that expects to die and be succeeded by his son.

At present, if a member is **disfellowshipped**, which involves being officially excommunicated and "sent to Coventry," he or she must be totally ignored. This action can create special difficulties when the shunned Witness happens to work or live with other Witnesses. Those that leave because they have concluded the Society is not teaching the truth are considered to be the most dangerous of all defectors.

The Society has changed its mind several times regarding the treatment of those who quietly leave the movement. The rules concerning the treatment of relatives who have left change more often. At present it is permissible to occasionally see a relative who has left, provided that they have not been disfellowshipped. If they have, then all affection is transferred to the congregation, who are in effect a family of substitute brothers and sisters.

Some Witnesses who have criticised others for seeing opposed children, have compromised themselves when faced with the same dilemma. They are clearly breaking the rules, and an elder could lose his position if it became generally known that he was seeing opposed children.

Would it not be better for them to question whether the Society have the right to make up these changing rules that lead them to live in fear of discovery? For a mother or father to strive for the goal of everlasting life on earth in a "new world," believing that as they achieve their goal, their son or daughter will die at the very hand of the God who is rewarding them, must cause severe emotional conflict, if they love their child.

It is not enough to just passively say that they cannot help what God does. To qualify for this reward they must approve of the slaughter, believing it to be "righteous and just." They must love this vengeful God with their "whole heart, mind and strength." Their literature describes at length how having witnessed the mass slaughter they will stand and applaud.

The Pool of Tears

It is hard to imagine the suffering that disfellowshipping can cause. Along with the belief that God himself has turned his back on the person concerned, leaving him or her in the dangerous position of expecting to be executed at Armageddon, is the isolation from all those they love when they need them the most. Their dearest and closest friends will not talk to them. In recent years the rules have been altered and it is permissible at the moment to acknowledge them if they say "hello," but who knows what the rules will be in the future?

If the disfellowshipped person wants to be reinstated they must continue to attend the meetings and sit quietly at the back. The other Witnesses, even those sitting next to them, are not allowed to speak to them. When the person has suffered months or sometimes years of this treatment, the elders may consider lifting the ban. If their sin has been smoking or fornication, then reinstatement can be fairly swift. By far the worst charge is that of apostasy, which to Witnesses means voicing doubts about their Society.

Elders can never be sure that someone guilty of their idea of apostasy has really had a change of heart. More than this, there is the risk of doubt spreading through the congregation and for this reason offenders are kept on ice for as long as possible.

The Society claims that the purpose of disfellowshipping is to bring the erring one to their senses but there is another motive. As the offenders are often guilty of apostasy, there is a need to keep others from speaking to them and actually finding that they may be speaking the truth. For this reason anyone who leaves by choice because they disagree with the Society, or has resigned out of principle, is labelled as an "evil one" and given the same treatment.

There is little chance of such a person wanting to return. The sole reason for refusing to see or speak to such a rebel is to stop the members hearing his or her viewpoint. The members left behind have to rely on a single statement announced by the elders to ascertain what has happened. Whether a member loses his or her friends as a result of resignation or disfellowshipping, the emotional cost can be high.

In my own case I was never disfellowshipped but slowly moved from the centre of the organization to the edge as I became more and more disillusioned. It took some years to fully come to terms with the fact that what I had accepted as truth for all my life was in fact flawed. I tried to stay and do the minimum required of a member to still be called a brother. In the end I could no longer live a lie and at the age of thirty, finally left the Kingdom Hall for the last time. Not one person ever called to ask why! They had realized from remarks I had made, that I had, in the words of the song, "come to doubt all that I once held as true."

Unlike so many others I was fortunate enough to have a wife who felt the same as me, and we left together and built a new life, with new friends and a different and happier outlook. I was never disfellowshipped or disassociated but my relatives, all of whom are Witnessess except one brother, continue to shun me.

I will never forget the friends and relatives whose affection I lost, along with the feeling of safety that belonging to the Watchtower Society's world brought me. All my life I had been promised that I would never grow old and die but would live forever on earth, when it was turned into a paradise. Now I realized that I was going to grow old and die like every other human. Coming to terms with the reality of so many wasted years and learning to live outside the organization and accept as worthwhile, people who I had previously condemned, was a long hard climb.

The following statements have been made by men and women who have left or been disfellowshipped and give a true life impression of the anguish this can bring :

I loved those people more than I can say. They were my friends, my family, and my whole world for 13 years. I believe with all my heart that they loved me too, and still do, as I love each of them. The thought of having my disagreements with Watchtower Society teachings discovered and being disfellowshipped and losing every one that ever meant anything to me was unbearable.

Miss D.F.

I typed a letter resigning my responsibilities. I handed it to the elders ... I was bitter after 24 years of my life in which I gave up all personal goals. Being a ninth grade dropout, I had to eke out a living with minimum wage jobs. Now I look back and wonder how stupid it all was. Yet, the worst was to happen. The strain on my family during all this time, caused by my own physical and emotional breakdown was immense. My wife carried all the weight as I went downhill. I could barely work: my nerves were bad. I had three sensitive sons who were very affected by seeing their father treated so poorly by those who claimed to love their dad. Michael was particularly disturbed by all of this. He went downhill to the point where he just broke down and could not trust anyone and just hated himself. We tried everything, psychiatrists to family therapy for help. We begged the elders to come over to pray for my family and me but they were so cold towards these kind of emotional problems. Finally on Nov. 17, 1981 Michael killed himself. He was 16.   Mr F.Z.

I was disfellowshipped in 1981 ... when I needed them the most, they turned their backs on me and my family. I was so dedicated to the organization that I fought the reality of what they were doing to me. Being thrown out hurt more than I could possibly say. I went downhill so fast that it all seems like a nightmare.   Name withheld

I am fourteen years old ... My whole family was disfellowshipped because of celebrating Christmas ... We did however go back to the Kingdom Hall for a meeting early last year. I was very shocked when I got there – all the people who used to be my friends, were now my enemies. The people who claimed to be so God-and-Christ like were just the opposite. They teach hatred and punishment, while God and Jesus teach forgiveness and love.   Miss R.L.S.

My sister, whom I love very much was disfellowshipped. I was not allowed to say one word to her. My mother is a Jehovah's Witness still, also my brother and sister-in-law. I was in such fear of that organization that I wouldn't dare to talk to her or be seen in public with her. My husband is also a Jehovah's Witness. He is very strict to the point that he chooses the organization over me, his own wife. We have four children and he insists they will be destroyed unless they go to the meetings with him. They are getting brainwashed. Now that I am disfellowshipped, my eleven year old son says, "I don't have to listen to her, she's just an apostate," and my husband doesn't do a thing; he goes along with him. They treat me like the dirt under the rug and that's not the half of it!   Mrs R.M

It's almost a year since I resigned from the Society. I do miss most of my family who are Witnesses, my friends, but not the tyranny control of the Society. MRS U.L.

Every single one of my relatives is one of Jehovah's Witnesses and not one has ever left or been disfellowshipped, ever! I have sixteen cousins, three great cousins, and five sets of aunts and uncles and of course grandparents. And I'm thinking of leaving. This is tearing me apart because although I'm not disfellowshipped or disassociated, none of my relatives will have anything to do with me. Neither do any of the Jehovah's Witnesses in town, because I haven't regularly attended the meetings since January. NAME WITHHELD

I was put on trial twice for apostasy as a Jehovah's Witness, and disassociated myself before they disfellowshipped me. I lived with my Jehovah's Witness husband for a year before our divorce (and experienced all of the agonizing shunning silence, and mistrust that went along with that) lost my family and oldest son because of shunning and on a weekly basis must cope with the emotional devastation that my youngest two children experience every time they visit their dad on the weekends and he tells them things like, "Mummy is going to die at Armageddon because she is not a Jehovah's Witness," etc. I well know the heartbreak caused by the Watchtower. MRS P.M

My heart is broken. My daughter has broken my heart in two with just a little piece holding it together. She let them do this to us, and shunned me, her mother, at her own wedding at my expense. Her old girlfriends were all there crying and sobbing. She told them they couldn't be in her wedding or come to theirs if in a church. I loved them; she threw them out of her life. I sobbed and sobbed. Sometimes I wish I could just die, it hurts so bad. My baby girl threw her brother out, hurt him so bad. My husband, is hurting to the bone with the way she let them treat our old friends. How can they call themselves Christians?
NAME WITHHELD

I left the group, but my daughter has remained a Jehovah's Witness. This would not be so bad except that Jehovah's Witnesses are not allowed to speak to one who quits, so I don't get to see Lauren any more. I don't get to visit and love my grandchildren because the Governing Body of Jehovah's Witnesses have told my family that I am wicked and evil and even demonized.

20 years I spent in the Watchtower Society – 3 years I have been out and after 3 years of terror and heartache I am now feeling the love of Jesus.   MRS W.B.

I cry buckets of tears daily for my family, therefore my message to you today:

Be careful when the Jehovah's Witnesses come to your door. Don't let them into your home or you might just lose your own little Lauren. But if they do come to your house, would you please do me a big favour? Would you tell them that if they happen to see Lauren ask her to phone home as her mother loves her dearly.   MRS G.N.

As you can see from the experiences you have read, despite the Society's safeguards and the pain involved some do leave the organization and prompt others to question the Society's claim to be the only Christian movement in the world. In view of this, the rules concerning association are unlikely to be relaxed. It is my belief that the years ahead will see an intensified effort to reduce contact with those who dare to question.

The Society would like its members to believe that the main reason for some leaving is that they become impatient with waiting for the promised end of this system, followed by a "new world." This is not the case. If someone believes that a new world is coming, then it makes little difference when it arrives.

We can all accept disappointment. What cannot be reconciled is the Society's denial that they were directly involved in the expectation that Armageddon was due to take place at any moment. This, coupled with a loss of confidence in the belief that the Society are who they claim to be, or that they are teaching "the truth", is the cause of many Witnesses leaving. To be a

Witness one must have total faith in the Society itself.

Doubt about the Society's sincerity led me to examine their history and beliefs in a way strongly discouraged by them – with good reason. The findings are in the following chapters.

The Watchtower Society have built an organization based on the invisible return of Christ, invisible fulfilment of prophecy upon a "spiritual nation," living in an invisible "spiritual paradise." These rewards that the members are so proud of can only be seen with the invisible "eyes of faith." I am left feeling like the little boy who, unable to go along with the pretence that the Emperor wore a fine suit of clothes, declared that the Emperor was as naked as the day that he was born.

Truth is not a rigid set of beliefs.
Once we think we possess the truth,
We close our mind to other possibilities,
In that moment we have suddenly,
Lost our connection with the infinite.

❋ ❋ ❋

5

LATE FOR A VERY IMPORTANT DATE

Pastor Russell's Society – 1887 to 1917

To fully understand why the Watchtower Society has found it necessary to adopt their present teachings we must go back to the early days of the movement.

A man named Charles Taze Russell, known as Pastor Russell, was born in 1852 in Pittsburg, America. He was a sincere man with a keen desire to understand the Bible. In 1879 he began to gather others with the same interest and by 1881 he had formed the original Watchtower Society. This group became known as "The International Bible Students." It would be many years before they adopted the name "Jehovah's Witnesses."

This small group who were sometimes referred to as Russellites, started to make predictions regarding the end of the world system. A book entitled *The Time is at Hand* followed in 1891. The title of this book emphasised the weakness that was to become a flaw in the Watchtower Society as the years passed – their obsession with time.

This book declared that Jesus Christ had already begun his presence since 1873 and would return to gather his chosen ones to heaven in 1914. Pastor Russell, along with his followers, expected to be taken to heaven to become part of Christ's heavenly priesthood and government in 1914. The battle of Armageddon was to follow and bring an end to all religious and political set-ups. This date was arrived at by various calculations and guesswork, designed to prove that the Gentile Times would end in 1914.

The Gentile Times being the time period that the non-Jewish nations would dominate the earth for.

> True it is expecting great things to claim, as we do, that within the coming twenty-six years all present governments will be over thrown and dissolved; but we are living in a special and peculiar time, the "Day of Jehovah," in which matters culminate quickly; and it is written, "A short work will the Lord make upon the earth."

> In view of the strong bible evidence concerning the times of the Gentiles, we consider it an established truth that the final end of the Kingdoms of this world and the full establishment of the Kingdom of God will be accomplished near the end of AD 1915. Then the prayer of the church, ever since her Lord took his departure – "Thy Kingdom Come" – will be answered; and under that wise and just administration, the whole earth will be filled with the glory of the Lord – with knowledge and right-eousness, and peace. (Psalms 72:19; Isaiah 6:3; Habakkuk 2:14) And Then The Will Of God Shall Be Done "On Earth As It Is In Heaven." THE TIME IS AT HAND – SERIES II – PAGES 98, 99

> Be not surprised, then when in subsequent chapters we present proofs that the setting up of God's Kingdom is already begun, that it is pointed out in prophecy as due to begin the "battle of the great day of God Almighty" (Revelation 16:14) which will end in AD 1915, with the complete overthrow of earth's present rulership, is already commenced. The gathering of the armies is plainly visible from the standpoint of God's word. PAGE 101

> In the preceding chapters we presented evidence showing that the "Times of the Gentiles" or their lease of domination, will run out with the year AD 1914 and at that time they will be overturned and Christ's Kingdom fully established. That the Lord must be present, and set up his Kingdom, and exercise great power so as to dash the Nations to pieces as a potters vessel, is then clearly fixed. PAGE 170

Pastor Russell understood that Christ's return would mean the restoration of Israel to their homeland as promised to Abraham.

An entire chapter, entitled "Parallel Dispensations" was devoted to providing scriptural proof that God had promised Israel would one day return to take possession of their land :

> But we must remember that the year AD 1878 was but the turning point of returning favour to fleshly Israel. We have already learned, from our study of "The Times of the Gentiles", that Jerusalem and its people will continue to be trodden down – controlled and oppressed by the Gentiles "until the Times of the Gentiles be fulfilled," and hence, though favour was due to begin in AD 1878, the Jew will not be received back into full favour until after 1915. PAGE 221

Large portions of the Old Testament were devoted to describing the return of Israel to their homeland as well as references in the New Testament. The Society's basic teachings were Bible based but went far beyond the things written in the Bible and claimed to know when these things would happen; also they claimed that only those in their group would go to heaven with Jesus.

They condemned all Christendom for refusing to agree with their time keeping. Many pages of this book were spent giving minute details of how these dates were arrived at, several charts were drawn and dozens of scriptural texts were manipulated into place to back up these predictions. *The Watchtower* magazine then known as *Zion's Watchtower* kept its readers up to date with world events. Social, financial and political events on an international scale were monitored and given Biblical significance.

In the following year *The Watchtower* magazine repeated the expectation :

> The date of the close of that "battle" is definitely marked in the Scriptures as October, 1914. It is already in progress, its beginning dating from October, 1874. THE WATCHTOWER – 15 JANUARY 1892

This prediction was repeated again two years later :

> We see no reason for changing the figures – nor could we change them if we would. They are, we believe, God's dates, not ours. Bear in mind that the end of 1914 is not the date for the beginning, but for the end of the time of trouble. We see no

49

reason for changing from our opinion expressed in the view presented in the *WATCH TOWER* of January 15,1892. We advise that it be read again.   THE WATCHTOWER – 15 JULY 1894

Needless to say 1914 passed without these things occurring. Conveniently for Pastor Russell, World War I broke out giving his Society something to point to as a major event arriving on schedule. The fact that he had not predicted such an event was not important – something had happened! This was to be used to great effect for decades to come.

The 1986 book *True Peace and Security* by the Watchtower Society says :

> As far back as 1876 Jehovah's Witnesses realized that bible prophecy marked the year 1914 CE as a time when major events would take place that would have far reaching effects on human affairs. They gave reason for this wide publicity. (Page 70)

Throughout the years and until this day they give all members the impression that they were entirely correct in their prophecies concerning 1914. Only those who take the trouble to read what was really said will know – they were entirely wrong! The Israelites did not return to their homeland. The members of the Society were not taken to heaven. Christ did not come and destroy all political and religious organizations. In a rare moment of honesty the Watchtower Society publication *Light Book I* (1930) admitted :

> All of the Lord's people looked forward to 1914 with joyful expectation. When that time came and passed there was much disappointment, chagrin and mourning and the Lord's people were greatly in reproach. They were ridiculed by the clergy and their allies in particular, and pointed to with scorn, because they had said so much about 1914, and what would come to pass, and their "prophecies" had not been fulfilled.   PAGE 194

Christians at that time had seen the Watchtower as the false prophet it had proved itself to be and quoted the Bible warning :

> The prophet who presumes to speak in my name a word that I have not commanded him to speak or who speaks in the name

of other gods, that prophet must die. And in case you should say in your heart: "How shall we know the word that Jehovah has not spoken?" when the prophet speaks in the name of Jehovah and the word does not occur or come true, that is the word that Jehovah did not speak. With presumptuousness the prophet spoke it. You must not get frightened at him.

DEUTERONOMY 18:20-22 – NWT

Impostors will come claiming to be messiahs or prophets, and they will produce great signs and wonders to mislead even God's chosen, if such a thing were possible. See, I have fore-warned you.

MATTHEW 24:23-25 – NE

By 1916 it was apparent that the date had not brought the fulfil-ment of these major prophecies. The book was reprinted with a foreword, which explained:

This was a natural mistake to fall into, but the Lord overruled it for the blessing of his people. The thought that the church would all be gathered to glory before 1914 certainly did have a stimulating and sanctifying effect upon thousands, all of whom accordingly can praise the Lord – even for the mistake. PAGE 1V

To "praise the Lord – even for the mistake" gave the impression that God was in some way involved in the false prophecy which the final paragraph in the book had called "an unquestionable certainty."

In 1917 Pastor Russell died having sold his family business and donated a total of $250,000 to the Society, a fortune in those days.

Judge Rutherford Takes Charge

Within two months Pastor Russell was replaced by Judge Rutherford. The appointment was not approved by many of the men who had faithfully worked under Pastor Russell. The Society's own book *Jehovah's Witnesses in the Divine Purpose* explains that whereas Pastor Russell had been, "kind warm and very tactful" Judge Rutherford had a tendency to be "brusk and direct ... a directness in his approach to problems in dealing with his "brothers" that caused some to take offence." (Page 68,69)

The seven men who comprised the Board of Directors thought that he had too much power. "Their idea was to make the President's position secondary to the Board of Directors and limit his authority to that of an advisor." (Page 70)

Four members of the Board agreed to this change. Before action was taken, Rutherford wrote and produced a new book *The Finished Mystery* to be released as the latest publication, without consulting the members of the Board. The opposing members of the Board were outraged and a five-hour row followed. Judge Rutherford used a legal technicality to dismiss from their positions, the four members of the Board who had been handpicked by Pastor Russell. From then on the Society was under the total control of Judge Rutherford.

The members who had been dismissed set up in opposition to Rutherford's Society and over the two years that followed, at least 4,000 members left, a sizeable portion of the movement. Rutherford claimed that this was in fulfillment of Bible prophecy, quoting from Matthew chapter 25, which talks of an unworthy slave being thrown out, he said :

> The power seeking ones and those dissatisfied with sincere efforts to conduct matters according to the Legal Charter and Bible principles were frustrated. They indulged in considerable "beating of their fellow slaves" in a verbal way in print and by word of mouth and in judicial court. They put themselves on the side of the "confirmed drunkards" of this world, spiritually speaking, especially during those days of World War I.
>
> GOD'S KINGDOM OF A THOUSAND YEARS – PAGE 360 – PAR. 62

The disputed book *The Finished Mystery* contained another prophecy:

> Also, in the year 1918 when God destroys the churches wholesale and the church members by the millions, it shall be that any that escape shall come to the works of Pastor Russell to learn the meaning of the downfall of Christianity.   PAGE 485

This prophecy also failed.

6

THE DORMOUSE GOES INTO THE TEAPOT

Punished for Falling Asleep – 1917 to 1925

Returning to the years leading up to 1919 the Society had many problems, resulting at one point in the publication of *The Watchtower* coming to a halt for the first time in forty years. Some thought this was the end of the Society. Eight of the leaders were given twenty-year prison sentences for violation of the Espionage Act. The Brooklyn Headquarters were closed down.

With World War I at its peak, feelings against the members were running high, owing to their refusal to join the War movement; also, their claim that all religions and governments, other than their own of course, are run by Satan the Devil. A series of attacks on individuals followed and the movement came to a standstill. A short time later the charges were reviewed and the leaders were released in 1919. This brief pause in the Society's printing activity and short imprisonment of its key figures is said to have fulfilled numerous Bible prophecies :

"The Kingdom of the heavens will become like ten virgins ... while the bridegroom was delayed they all nodded and went to sleep." (Matthew 25:1-5) This nodding and falling asleep is said to be a pictorial prophecy concerning the chosen ones of Jehovah's Witnesses who, disappointed that Jesus had not returned in 1914, fell asleep spiritually. As a penalty for their sleepy attitude, Jehovah God saw to it that the Watchtower leaders were punished with imprisonment. They explain :

> In 1919, following the release of eight prominent members of the Watchtower Bible and Tract Society from unjust imprisonment, it was the due time for the virgin classes to be aroused from their sleepy inactivity. The work of worldwide enlightenment lay ahead.
>
> BOOK – WORLDWIDE SECURITY UNDER THE PRINCE OF PEACE. PAGE 41

The virgins in the Bible prophecy, whose lamp oil had run out, while they were asleep, were said to be the members who had left because they disagreed with the way Judge Rutherford was running the Society.

A master gives money to his servants to speculate with while he is away. One slave hides his money in the ground and makes no profit for his master so when the master returns he throws him out. (Matthew 25:13-30) The money is said to represent a commission given to the Society to gain converts. The lazy slave, who made no profit, is supposed to represent those who left Rutherford and any who leave now. It is also said to represent all Christian clergymen.

"Strike the shepherd and let those of the flock be scattered; and I shall certainly turn my hand back upon those who are insignificant." (Zechariah 13:7 NWT) This prophecy is referring to Israel. The Society claims that they are the flock scattered during the War years and re-gathered in 1919. As usual they "did not then appreciate that it was being fulfilled on them then." (*God's Kingdom of a Thousand Years* – Page 352) This prophecy actually refers to the death of Christ as the shepherd. (Clearly shown in Matthew 26:31)

Jesus cleanses the temple. (Malachi 3:1-5) This scriptural text is also claimed and applied to 1919.

"Many of them that sleep in the dust of the earth shall wake up, some to everlasting life, some to reproaches and eternal abhorrence."(Daniel 12:2 NE) This is said to refer to the Witnesses of Jehovah God as "laying dead in the very streets of this worldly organization. They were as asleep in death."

A mighty king persecutes God's holy ones for 3½ times.

(Daniel 7:23-28) Also said to refer to the three and a half years of difficulty the Society experienced.

The removal of "the continual sacrifice by the desolating abomination." (Daniel 12:11) This is generally thought to be a reference to the Roman armies destroying the temple in Jerusalem and ending the Jewish custom of animal sacrifices. The Society claim that the removal of sacrifice also refers to their imprisonment. The abomination – The League of Nations set up in 1919.

> The hand of the lord came upon me and he carried me out by his spirit and put me down in a plain full of bones ... these bones are the whole people of Israel ... I will open your graves and bring you up from them, and restore you to the land of Israel.   EZEKIEL 37:1,11-13 NE

This is a straightforward prophecy repeating the Biblical promise to restore Israel to its land – again the Society says this is another reference to them and their release from prison in 1919.

"... the Lord himself will descend from heaven; first the Christian dead will rise, then we who are left shall join them, caught up in the clouds to meet the Lord in the air." (1 Thessalonians 4:16,17 NE) Yes, once again this text is claimed and applied to the re-launch of the Watchtower Society in 1919 :

> In that first post war period there was an awakening from the inactive death like state. The sanctuary class wanted to be alive and expend their strength, time and means giving a worldwide witness to establish God's Kingdom.
> YOUR WILL BE DONE ON EARTH – PAGE 326

These and other scriptural texts from many different Bible books are taken by the Watchtower Society and applied to the imprisonment and release of eight men in America. Was the whole Bible, with all its prophets and apostles, really written with 1919 and the Watchtower Society in mind? May I suggest you read the texts I have cited in your own Bible, in full, to see whether their context allows for such an application?

One of the most important dates in the Society's history is

1919. Whether the Society's claim that these Bible prophecies were fulfilled on them, makes any sense, is of vital importance. If it is decided that these scriptures cannot be applied in this way, then the entire basis for their movement collapses.

Is it feasible that all these Bible prophecies, and many more not shown here, could really apply exclusively to a handful of men in America in 1919? It is even less likely when we remember that much of the information being printed by them at the time was inaccurate and is no longer believed by the present day Society.

The Society's intense introspection has distorted their perspective. At that time the world was preoccupied with the greatest war it had so far experienced. The terrible conditions many suffered on the battlefields, coupled with the maimed casualties returning home, left the powers that be with very little time to worry about eight men in jail in America many miles from the war zone.

World War I ended and the most difficult time in the Watchtower Society was behind them. Rather than taking up a Christian ministry they renewed their campaign against all religious and political establishments. The difficulties they had been through were once again claimed to be in direct fulfilment of Bible prophecy. The same technique of taking obscure Biblical texts and applying them to themselves was employed to the full.

Two witnesses/prophets who had tormented those on earth are killed and laid in the open. After three and a half days they are resurrected and taken to heaven. (Revelation chapter 11) These two prophets are supposed to be the Watchtower Society or Jehovah's Witnesses as they later became and their death, the state of inactivity during the war years, the three and a half days. As the Witnesses were taken to heaven it is claimed that all members of their "heavenly class" who had already died were taken to heaven in 1919. From then on any in this "class" who die, immediately go to heaven to rule with Christ. This class, strictly limited to 144,000, is based on the Biblical Revelation to John. Witnesses will often refer to this class as

"The 144,000."

They even go as far as to compare the lull in their printing activity to the terrible death Jesus is believed to have suffered :

Hence the expression "The Great City" must mean the antitypical unfaithful Jerusalem, namely Christendom. Certainly "in a spiritual sense she can be called Sodom and Egypt," and it was primarily in the midst of her that God's "two witnesses" were killed in 1918 CE just as their Lord, Jesus Christ was killed on a stake at unfaithful Jerusalem in 33 CE, so his followers, God's "two witnesses," the anointed were killed in Christendom.

Every detail of this chapter was given an application. (A full account is found in the Watchtower book *Then is Finished the Mystery of God* chapter 19 – Death and Resurrection of the Two Witnesses. The above quote is found on page 273)

As the few examples above show, Jehovah's Witnesses believe that most of the Bible was written about them and their activities. People who debate with them are often impressed by how well they know their Bibles. They seem to be able to explain the meaning of every Bible text and claim that their ability to interpret the whole Bible is proof that their Society is God's sole channel of communication with humans. There will be many more examples of their unique gift as you read on. You will be able to form your own opinion about the truth of their claim.

No Heaven For the Righteous

The Watchtower Society quickly recovered and true to its form began to prophesy again. A new date for Armageddon was set:

"The date 1925 is even more distinctly indicated than 1914."
THE WATCHTOWER JANUARY – 1922 – PAGE 22

The booklet *Millions Now Living Will Never Die* written in 1920 stated under the heading "Earthly Rulers" :

As we heretofore stated, the great jubilee is due to begin in 1925. At that time the earthly phase of the Kingdom shall be recognised. The Apostle Paul in the eleventh chapter of Hebrews

57

names a long list of faithful men who died before the crucifixion of the Lord and before the bringing of the selection of the church. These can never be a part of the heavenly class; they had no heavenly hopes; but God has in store something good for them. They are to be resurrected as perfect men and constitute the princes or rulers of the earth according to his promise (Psalm 45:16; Isaiah 32:1; Matthew 8: 11) therefore we may confidently expect that 1925 will mark the return of Abraham, Isaac, Jacob and the faithful prophets of old, particularly those named by the Apostle in Hebrews chapter eleven, the condition of human perfection.   PAGES 88 & 89

The Society had decided that the Bible's faithful men of old including Abraham would not go to heaven. They had reserved this hope for themselves. Not only were they going to heaven but also they were to be Kings and Priests with Jesus.

Members around the world spread the word and eagerly looked forward to Armageddon and the return of the faithful men of old. As late as 1924 the Society maintained the anticipation and repeated their prophecy :

We should therefore expect shortly after 1925 to see the awakening of Able, Enoch, David, Abraham, Jeremiah, Ezekiel, Daniel, John the Baptist, and others mentioned in the eleventh chapter of Hebrews.   *THE WAY TO PARADISE* – PAGE 224

"Millions now living will never die,"

was to become an enduring slogan that would be repeated many times over the coming years. The slogan was again used in the 1990's but overlooked the fact that most of the Society's members who had first heard it in 1920 had died of old age. This inspiring slogan had proved to be another false utterance.

The Same Promise

To this day the membership is still waiting for the men of faith to return to earth. Their belief is based on the idea that all men of faith who lived before the time of Christ cannot share in a

heavenly hope. Such men and women are expected to live forever on earth with the majority of the Witnesses.

As Abraham, or Abram lived before the time of Christ he put
faith in his God, Jehovah, as he believed that this was the requirement for gaining eternal life. "And he put faith in Jehovah; and
he proceeded to count it to him as righteousness." (Genesis 15:6
– NWT)

The Witnesses state that Abraham, along with all other faithful men who lived prior to the birth of Christ, can only ever hope
to live on earth when it is restored to a paradise.

Did Abraham believe he would go to heaven?

In Hebrews chapter eleven, Apostle Paul explains the meaning
of his faith, and what he believed the reward for that faith to be,
as demonstrated by Abraham and other men of his time. They
were temporary residents because they were seeking a place in
heaven.

> "All these persons died in faith. They were not yet in possession
> of the things promised, but had seen them far ahead and hailed
> them, and confessed themselves no more than strangers or
> passing travellers on earth. Those who use such language show
> plainly that they are looking for a country of their own. If their
> hearts had been in the country they had left, they could have
> found opportunity to return. Instead, we find them longing for
> a better country – I mean the heavenly one. That is why God is
> not ashamed to be called their God; for he has a city ready for
> them." (Hebrews 11:13-16 – NE) The Witnesses own Bible reads:
> "But now they are reaching out for a better (place), that is, one
> belonging to heaven."

Paul goes onto list many men of old and their acts of faith, ending by explaining that due to their faith they would reach perfection in company with the apostles :

> These also, one and all, are commemorated for their faith; and
> yet did not get to enter upon the promised inheritance, with us
> in mind, God had made a better plan, that only in company

with us should they reach their perfection. VERSE 40

Consequently those who adhere to faith are being blessed together with faithful Abraham. Moreover, if you belong to Christ, you are really Abraham's seed, heirs with reference to a promise. GALATIANS 3:9, 29 NWT

Now we, brothers, are children belonging to the promise the same as Isaac was. GALATIANS 4:28 NWT

But I tell you that many from eastern parts and western parts will come and recline at the table with Abraham and Isaac and Jacob in the kingdom of the heavens. MATTHEW 8:11 NWT

Christians believe they will be blessed together with Abraham, Isaac and the faithful men of old. To them Abraham is the pioneer or father of all those having the Christian faith.

7

A NEW NATION

Claim to Fame – 1925 to 1960

As time passed, the Society realized that their predictions were not going to come true. To say that their understanding of the Bible was correct, but that their timing was out would be one possible way of saving face. But to admit this would make a mockery of all the literature published over the previous forty years. And what of the damning statements made against those who had always said they were twisting the scriptures; also their claim to be guided by God would be disproved.

Judge Rutherford came up with the answer. He claimed that Jesus had returned in 1914 and was ruling in the heavens – but invisibly! Only with the aid of the Society's books would any-one be able to see this, as Jesus was revealing himself through them. But did not the Bible state that when Jesus returned Israel would go back to its homeland even as the Society had so far taught, stating as late as 1924 that Jerusalem would become the capital of the world?

It was at this point that the entire understanding of the Bible, as taught by the Watchtower Society, did a somersault.

Judge Rutherford explained that the followers of the Society had replaced Israel and all the blessings promised to Israel were to be bestowed on them. All Bible references to Israel were a coded way of foretelling the rise of Jehovah's Witnesses, though at that time they had still not adopted this name. Due to their rejection of Jesus, Israel was to be cast away forever. This was in total contrast to the entire chapter in *The Time is at Hand* entitled

"Parallel Dispensations," where by quoting many scriptures they had attempted to show that Israel, as an earthly nation, had been promised that it would return to God's favour and its homeland.

Many of the books written from then, set out to prove that all the promises made in the Bible, relating to Israel, had been or were about to be fulfilled on the Society and its followers.

The Witnesses now believed that they alone were God's chosen people. They alone had God's spirit and guidance. Israel was restored – the Witnesses were living proof! The Bible's promise to bring Israel into a land of their own where they would dwell in peace and security had been fulfilled. The Jehovah's Witnesses now believed they were Israel restored.

The Bible says that the desert around Israel would blossom and fresh water would spring from parched ground. The desert was said to be the state of spiritual need the churches had kept people in. Now the information in the Society's books and more specifically their Watchtower magazine was the fresh water.

> In contrast with the dilapidated religious condition of Christendom, honest observers of the spiritual estate of Jehovah's Witnesses have been obliged to exclaim: " The land yonder which was laid desolate has become like the garden of Eden."
>
> THE NATIONS SHALL KNOW THAT I AM JEHOVAH – PAGE 331

The promises of Israel gathering gold and silver were merely pictorial and referred to the richness of Jehovah's Witnesses, as they now had the priceless information provided through their Society. The Watchtower was now "The City of Refuge" which Israelites must go to for protection. It was a modern day "Noah's Ark". It was, and still claims to be, God's one and only organization.

> For instructions issue from Zion and out of Jerusalem come the word of the Lord; He will judge between nations, arbiter among many peoples. They shall their swords into mattocks and their spears into pruning knives, nation shall not lift sword against nation nor ever be trained for war.   ISAIAH 2:3,4 NE

These instructions from Zion were said to come through the Society. They claimed that they had fulfilled this scripture, as they were conscientious objectors during World War I.

For Israel to be permanently abandoned, as the Witnesses claim, the promise to Abraham would have to be broken. The Witnesses claim that God has done this to make way for them. However the Bible states that he would not cast Israel away forever. Most of the Old Testament and some of the New is written about Israel, ending with the achievement of God's original purpose, to restore Israel to favour. According to the Bible, he has sworn to do this! The promise to Israel is repeated throughout the New Testament, which states that the old covenant was abandoned for the sake of Israel, but Israel itself was to be saved.

The Apostle Paul likens Israel to a tree and shows that those who have come into favour in place of Israel are like branches that have been grafted on. He explains that it is because Israel is the root that these branches are made holy :

> I ask then, has God rejected his people? I cannot believe it! I am an Israelite myself, of the stock of Abraham, of the tribe of Benjamin. No! God has not rejected the people which he acknowledged of old as his own.

> For there is a deep truth here, my brothers ... this partial blindness has come upon Israel only until the Gentiles have been admitted in full strength; when that has happened the whole of Israel shall be saved, in agreement with the text of scripture ...
>
> ROMANS CHAPTER 11

It is best to read the whole chapter rather than the abbreviated text shown, to see if it is feasible that the promises concerning Israel have been fulfilled through Jehovah's Witnesses. This pictorial language was from then on to be applied at every opportunity and lead to a complicated application of every Bible book and prophecy. Anything to do with Israel really meant the Witnesses.

As the years passed, the need to make all the pieces fit into this new jigsaw was to lead to constant changes and revisions.

A detailed dissection of otherwise straightforward Bible prophecies followed in order to make the entire Bible appear to be written for the Witnesses. Each interpretation was labelled a "new truth." To this day, despite numerous alterations, this format is still used.

The Watchtower Society were then able to claim that without their books it is impossible to understand the Bible. Well, it is true that without their books no one would ever come to the understanding they place on scripture.

The Nation Needs Laws

The nation of Israel had many laws to keep, on pain of death. Now the Society claimed to be a new nation, replacing Israel, they decided they too must have laws.

As the years passed more and more rules or laws were introduced. Failure to comply with these laws meant rejection from their nation, the equivalent of death in their eyes. They referred to their magazine as Zion's Watchtower. Later, their own translation of the Bible was to render "For instruction issues from Zion." as "For out of Zion law will go forth." (Isaiah 2:3) The Society decided on these laws themselves claiming that they were God's mouthpiece.

From their earliest days the Society were adept at adapting scripture to support every claim made. They drew detailed charts with dates and were able to quote scripture to make every prediction and interpretation appear irrefutable. To the uninformed reader the abundance of scriptural quotations, cleverly intermingled with their own application, gave an impressive account of the Society's authenticity.

As so many of these "understandings" have now been altered, we must ask - what became of the "scriptural proof" used to back them up? Why did God make such a mess of communicating to the world through his only channel of communication?

In 1930 a house was built in San Diego, California, and named "Bethsarim" meaning "House of the Princes." The house, set in a hundred acres of land and lived in by Judge Rutherford, was acquired to accommodate the patriarchs when they returned to earth. They were still expected, but just a little late.

The Advantages of Hindsight

If Jesus did return in 1914, why did no one see him? Even the Witnesses, then known as "Bible Students," were still waiting for him to come in 1918. Not until years later in 1929, did the Society "realize" that Jesus had returned in 1914 and that they had failed to notice! Despite expecting Jesus, they missed him.

Did the Bible say that Jesus would not be noticed even by his chosen nation of Jehovah's Witnesses when he returned?

> **"Behold, he is coming with the clouds!**
> **Every eye will see him ... "** Revelation 1:7 NE

Whether this reference is meant to refer to the literal eye or not, there is no doubt that according to the Bible, Jesus will make himself known. The Watchtower Society overcame this discrepancy by saying that Jesus returned in a sense in 1914 to take up his presence invisibly. He then came again in 1919, also invisibly, to take the deceased members of the Society to heaven. They had originally taught that Jesus had returned in 1873.

They are still waiting for his third return, which is said to be any day now. This return will be noticed by the world.

This convenient way of using Bible prophecy is a pattern that occurs many times. Invisible or symbolic so far, literal and seen by everyone – always a day away. Did the Bible really predict that Jesus would return this many times, and why did the Witnesses miss him the first time, only realising with hindsight that he had visited?

The Faithful and Discreet Slave

The Society sought further authority by adopting more Biblical texts.

> Who really is the faithful and discreet slave whom the master appointed over his domestics, to give them food at the proper time. Matthew 24:45 – NWT

Many in the Society had always believed the "faithful slave" to be Pastor Russell. Now this singular slave was said to comprise the changing group who wrote the literature, the Governing Body. This was the "food given at the proper time." However anyone who opposed the Society's teachings or wanted to hold with previous Society "truths" was labelled an "evil slave".

As individuals, they could be labelled as "evil slaves" and thrown out. All members can become "evil slaves" but only those chosen by the Society can become "faithful slaves." To this day, those in charge, the Governing Body, refer to themselves as the **"faithful and discreet slave."** When the movement is doing well they are "increasing the King's belongings" as the faithful slave had done. When there are problems, the evil slave is responsible.

A Name for the New Nation

In keeping with their new status as the restored nation of Israel, in 1931, the Society decided to claim further authority by their use of scripture. "Ye are my Witnesses," saith the Lord, "and my servant whom I have chosen:" (Isaiah 43:10 – King James)

It was from this time on that the former Bible Students became known as **Jehovah's Witnesses**. The adoption of this title was a shrewd move. The Bible contains many references to Witnesses, and now these scriptures could be given a direct application. This was to be used to the full. Later their own version of the Bible was to render the previously quoted scripture :

> **"You are my Witness," is the utterance of Jehovah, "even my servant whom I have chosen ... "** ISAIAH 43:10 – NWT

It could now be claimed that far from being a new religion, Jehovah's Witnesses were in fact the oldest religion in the world to worship the God of the Bible.

In the book entitled *The New World*, Abel, Noah and Moses are named in person and claimed as Jehovah's Witnesses, also Job :

> It is the proper time, therefore, to consider carefully the life history of Job, who was a Witness for Jehovah God. His true life experience was a prophetic drama which exposes the war hotly waged by religion against Jehovah's Witnesses from and after Abel, the first martyr slain by a religionist.   PAGE 130 (1942)

Job, who was now a Jehovah's Witness, was still late returning, but not forgotten :

> The scriptural and physical facts prove that Job is due to be resurrected shortly with those faithful men to appear on earth with them ... those faithful men of old may be expected back any day now. The scriptures give us good reason to believe that it shall be shortly before Armageddon breaks.
>
> PAGES 104 & 130

In the book entitled *Jehovah's Witnesses in the Divine Purpose* further fascinating claims are made. The first chapter – "A People with a most Ancient History"– states :

> Jesus himself was a member of this ancient Jewish nation and he was one of Jehovah's Witnesses ... No greater Witness than Jesus ever lived on earth, and one of his apostles specifically called Jesus a Witness ... Do you mean to say, then, that Jesus' disciples were Witnesses too? Certainly. Christians are urged to emulate all those ancient Witnesses that preceded them back to Able.
>
> 1959

The adoption of the name Jehovah's Witnesses was another example of scripture being applied with the benefit of hindsight.

Jehovah not Jesus

The Watchtower Society had originally referred to Jesus as their Lord, and as with all Christian religions looked to him as their leader. Now they had adopted a new name, less and less reference was made to Jesus as Lord, but attention was slowly directed to Jehovah. This is one translation of the Hebrew name that the Israelites used, though not the most accurate rendering.

Over the years the divine name was to be used more and more, leading to the publishing of The Watchtower Society's own translation of the Bible in 1950, which placed great emphasis on the name Jehovah. Jesus was given less and less credit. The Christian churches were criticised for their attention to Jesus instead of the Father Jehovah. This bias has continued until the present day.

The Bible calls Jesus "King of kings and Lord of lords" and states that he will personally come with his angels to claim his right to rule the earth. The Society in their book, *Worldwide Peace and Security Under the Prince of Peace* refer to Jesus as "field marshal." We are told under the heading "Jehovah's name beautified" :

> Thus, Jehovah of Armies by means of his field marshal Jesus Christ, will gain undying glory for himself surpassing anything that was described in *The book of the Wars of Jehovah* and in the Hebrew scriptures of the Holy Bible. How beautiful a name will Jehovah make for himself by his awe-inspiring victory in "the war of the great day of God Almighty!" "Jubilantly all lovers of that name will then laud it forever, singing forth his praises!"
>
> Forward, then, into battle action O Jehovah of armies, with your royal son at your side! PAGES 159, 160 (1986)

This is all designed to detract attention away from Jesus. The Society have in many ways presumed to take the place that Jesus holds in the minds of most Christians. Instead of looking to Jesus as the only way to salvation, they claim that only by joining and following them can one have a relationship with God. This means that all members are personally answerable to them. For a member to fall out with the Society would mean the end of their relationship with God.

The Great Crowd

Up until 1935, the Society had claimed that their entire membership would go to heaven, and quoted from Revelation 7:4 to show that the literal number of 144,000 would go to heaven.

As the number of members passed 60,000 they realized the need to allow for expansion. They achieved this in 1935 by announcing that, in addition to the chosen few there was also a "great multitude or crowd" who would not go to heaven, but grow to human perfection and live forever on earth with the resurrected men of old.

This idea was based on a "new truth" regarding their interpretation of Revelation 7:9 which refers to a **"great crowd"**. This great crowd could not have any direct communication with God, but could only gain salvation through association with the chosen ones in the Society. Thus they now claimed to have replaced Jesus as the only way to salvation.

From this time on, most Witnesses could only look forward to life on earth. They could only be granted everlasting life by total obedience to the Society. They were to follow its dictates to the letter. If they in any way questioned its decisions or interpretations, they would be expelled.

As there were now two classes, one with a belief that they would live forever on earth, the other with a heavenly hope, how would anyone know which class they were in? The directors at head office decided that they themselves would go to heaven, and in line with this status, retained their title of elder. Each congregation had until then, been run by members who had been voted in to the position of elder, by the other congregation members. They were now stripped of this title, and told that all congregations were to be run by company servants appointed by head office.

The Society had, in one move, taken away these men's positions as elders chosen by each congregation, and at the same time the hope of heavenly life for nearly all the members. This position was now reserved for the directors. In view of the higher class they were now in, they would make all future decisions regarding congregation matters. This gave the Society total control. To this day all members of the Governing Body claim to belong to the group with a heavenly hope. Finding suitable candidates of this calling to replace those who leave or pass away, has contributed to the drop in the number of men in the Governing Body from 18 to 13 at present. These men consider themselves to be the "faithful and discreet slave" that Jesus is said to have returned to gather from 1914. What is curious is that the latest member was not born until 1941, or baptised until 1959!

Needless to say, the members who had loyally devoted their lives to the organization were deeply hurt. The Watchtower Society had come a long way from their original roots as a sincere group of Bible students, under the direction of Pastor Russell. Too far for many – and they left as they had done ten years earlier in 1925, when the date for Armageddon had again proved to be a false prophecy.

Prison Bonds

Having made so much capital out of the few years some of the members had spent in prison during the War years, up until 1919, the Society realized the publicity that could be achieved by clashing with the authorities. Coupled with the growing suspicion among outsiders that the Society was a moneymaking organization, they decided to embark on a campaign against the courts.

The Witnesses were supposed to individually obtain permits to sell their books, so they broke the law and sold them without the permits. Whenever a Witness was arrested for this offence, the Society would take up the case. They argued that book selling was a part of their worship and refused to comply. To obtain permits would classify them as commercial booksellers and incur a tax liability.

This publicly gave the impression that they were being persecuted for their religion. Public sympathy and interest helped to increase book sales. One of the techniques used was to swamp a city with Witnesses all selling books without permits. The number arrested would overfill the jails and cause uproar. The Society would pre-arrange for the press to be present at these publicity stunts.

To increase the impression of persecution they adopted the slogan, "Religion is a Snare and a Racket." The anger this generated among some religious people led to mob violence.

The Society's law-breaking activity was highly organized and a special squad numbering 12,600 was formed. When the Witnesses were arrested, they would phone the nearest division who would go into action. The areas designated for these protests were called "Hot Spots."

During 1936, 1,149 Witnesses were charged in court for disturbing the peace and selling books without a permit. Court case by court case, the issue was fought all the way up to the American Supreme Court. A few years later the Witnesses won the right to sell their books and literature without a licence, as part of their worship.

The Watchtower Society claimed that this was a miracle – which summed up the feelings of their critics.

Bethsarim

When Judge Rutherford died in 1942, it was his wish to be buried in the grounds of his home "Bethsarim." The planning commission refused to allow this. This led to the Society printing an article under the presumptuous title "San Diego Officials line up against Earth's New Princes." It reads in part :

> The record of this whole affair is so outrageous that it is brought to public attention as disclosing the depth of meanness resorted to by religionists to satisfy their vindictiveness even on lifeless bones. It also furnishes a perfect example of those ensnared by religion. They have throw away all worthiness of life merely for the brief satisfaction of spite.

Here the Society publicly judged and condemned these officials. They decided that they were not worthy of life because they refused to issue a permit for burial on private land!

The house Bethsarim and its grounds had been acquired for Abraham and the other faithful men of old, who were originally expected to return in 1925. By 1950 they had still not appeared. The Society's own book *Jehovah's Witnesses and the Divine Purpose* recalls how the Society overcame this failed prophecy with an announcement at their international convention :

> Because of the understanding of this text that had prevailed for so long, many of Jehovah's Witnesses expected at every convention to greet Abraham, Isaac, Jacob, David and the others, welcoming them back from the dead. You can imagine, then, the electrifying effect on the audience this statement of the speaker made: "Would this international assembly be happy to know HERE, TONIGHT, in our midst, there are a number of prospective PRINCES OF THE NEW EARTH?"   PAGE 252

Thunderous applause ensued. This was a trick! No faithful men of old had reappeared. The speaker, Mr. Franz, then explained that there was nothing that scripturally argues against Christ's making many of these "other sheep" (those in the audience) "princes in the earth" as required. Thunderous applause again interrupted his momentous speech.

The Society had now decided that some of the earth's future princes could come from among its ordinary members – when the "new world" came. This "blessing" distracted the members from the fact that the long awaited men of faith had not appeared. It cost the Society nothing to reveal this "new truth" because appointment as a prince depended on the "new world" coming.

The real positions of authority, there and then, were still reserved for those behind the closed doors of the Society's offices. To date, none of those who gave the thunderous applause have been made princes. In fact a large number of them have passed away, despite counting themselves among the "millions now living who will never die."

World War II

The outbreak of World War II brought a wave of persecution against Jehovah's Witnesses, because of their refusal to be any part of the war movement. In Germany, the members were singled out for mistreatment. Hitler vowed to exterminate them. The stand they made for their beliefs and the courage they showed, has to be admired. Their refusal to fight was based on the belief that Christians are not allowed to show any partiality to political or national groups.

World War II was however not an entirely political exercise. Hitler was out to destroy the fundamental rights and liberty of all people, including the right to worship freely. Many Christians felt it was their duty to stand against what they saw as an evil force. When the allies got through to the concentration camps and liberated them, the survivors–Jehovah's Witnesses included – thanked God and felt their prayers had been answered. Those soldiers were fighting for more than their country.

The Society recently stated :

In this 20th century Jehovah has delivered his people from oppressions, bannings, persecutions and concentration camps. Like those boasting Assyrians of Isaiah's time, the Nazi ruler Adolf Hitler railed against Jehovah's Witnesses, on one occasion screaming, "This brood will be exterminated in Germany!" But it was Hitler and his Nazis that were exterminated. And now the small group of German Witnesses that trusted in Jehovah have grown to over 121,200!

THE WATCHTOWER – 15 JANUARY 1988

It is not consistent for the Witnesses to thank God for their deliverance and at the same time judge and condemn the men who liberated them, along with the church leaders. Liberation almost always involves force or the threat of force. The Witnesses state that if no one had fought in the war, there would have been no fighting. In an ideal world this would be the case, but as long as there are aggressors, even in the minority, people as family groups or nations may at times find it necessary to act in self-defence. It is only possible for minority groups, such as the Witnesses, to separate themselves from the struggles and conflicts of the human race.

It is important to realize that the Witnesses do not object to war with all its horrors. Their publications are filled with vivid descriptions of battles, past and future, and praise "Jehovah of Armies." They refer to him as their "Warrior God." In their book *Worldwide Security under the Prince of Peace*, a whole chapter is devoted to a gruesome description of the battle of Armageddon. Even Apostle John is involved :

Like a war correspondent, the apostle John gives an advanced account of the smashing victory that Jehovah's Field Marshal will gain in "the war of the great day of God the Almighty."

CHAPTER 19, PAGE 154 (1986)

Jehovah's Witnesses are not pacifists and do not object to war and bloodshed. If they thought it to be God's will, they would gladly take up arms and join in the predicted battle of Armageddon. Their objection to joining the army is that it is not in keeping with their ideals or the political cause that they support.

73

If attacked in their homes they would kill to defend their families. It has been claimed, by non-Witnesses, that the World War II war effort was an advanced measure to stop that necessity arising, that it was self-defence on a national scale.

Nevertheless, there are many aspects of war that do contradict the Christian principle of love for our fellow man. Jehovah's Witnesses are not alone in their view that the motive behind most wars fought among nations is greed. Political and commercial considerations are always involved. The sale of arms is a major money making business. Books have been written exposing the men behind the arms race and the vast profits made.

To those who feel strongly that war is wrong, and that the involvement of the Christian Church in war is against the teachings of Christ, the stand made by the Witnesses on this issue is their main reason for joining the movement.

The Watchtower Society and its members survived World War II. With so many people caught in the aftermath and worried about the future, disillusioned and in many cases bereaved, the Society seemed to have all the answers. The promise of living in a peaceful paradise earth with no war, loved ones to be resurrected and all to come any day, was an attractive package. People were looking for an alternative and the Watchtower Society offered it.

The annual production of *The Watchtower* magazine went from 18 million to 86 million copies in just twelve years. Numerous books were printed and by 1958 798,000 active members were reporting the time they spent selling literature. They were now a powerful organization. The many thousands of people involved in the production and distribution of this literature received no payment for their efforts.

The Society had successfully fought in the courts to establish the right to sell books without a licence. They were now a highly successful international publishing company owning many of their own printing works.They had survived two World Wars, opposition from "evil slaves" and had managed to flourish. They were now ready to move ahead.

8

PAINTING THE ROSES

The Divine Purpose – 1960 to 1990

The 1959 book, *Jehovah's Witnesses in the Divine Purpose*, previously quoted from, was an attempt by the Society to rewrite their own history in a favourable light. They talked in great detail about 1925, but amazingly made no reference to the huge build-up to this year or the large number that had left after yet another disappointment.

Two chapters devoted to the approach of 1914, made no reference at all to the predictions they had spent forty years making concerning this year. The closest they got to it was the deliberately vague comment:

> So these early watchers were reasonably certain of some of the things that were due to take place when 1914 arrived. Exactly how these prophecies were to be fulfilled was not altogether clear, but evidences were increasing steadily that this was to be a marked date in earth's history. PAGE 53

Partial quotes from Watchtower magazines were carefully cited, leaving out the specific prophecies that had been made. Anyone recently joining the movement would be left with the impression that the Watchtower Society had never made a mistake or alteration in their teachings, but had always foretold the future with startling accuracy – with God's help of course!

The older publications that contained the false prophecies, were not readily available to new members, and the seasoned Witnesses, loyal to the Society, would never discuss "old truths" with them. As previously stated, an "old truth" is the official name given to previously held beliefs that turned out to be false.

Many years later in 1972, the Society, eager to accuse others of false prophecy made the following statement. Their own words, intended to apply to others, sum up their own failings with startling accuracy:

> Jehovah the God of the true prophets will put all false prophets to shame either by not fulfilling the false prediction of self-assuming prophets or by having his own prophecies fulfilled in a way opposite to that predicted by false prophets. False prophets will try to hide their reasons for feeling shame by denying who they really are. They will try to avoid being killed or pronounced spiritually dead by Jehovah's loyal worshippers ... they would place love of God and his inspired word above all personal friendships with fleshly relatives or associates.
>
> PARADISE RESTORED TO MANKIND – BY THEOCRACY – PAGES 353, 354

Yes! These really are the Watchtower Society's own words. Many loyal and high-ranking Jehovah's Witnesses have come to view the Watchtower Society as a false prophet and left the organization, leaving behind their relatives, friends and associates. Sometimes the price of freedom and truth can be high, but what price is to be paid for denying truth?

The Time has Come

We have seen how the Watchtower Society overcame the failure of their original prophecies by claiming that all they had foretold had been fulfilled, but not in a literal way as expected. All fulfilment of prophecy was now either figurative or invisible. Only by reading their literature could anyone know that Bible prophecy was being fulfilled around them.

In the years that followed 1960, the membership increased beyond the Society's dreams. More and more books were printed and ten million Watchtower magazines were printed fortnightly in over a hundred languages. Increased revenue meant expansion, newer printing presses and more branches around the world. They claimed that this was further proof that God himself was directing the organization – his only channel of communication.

They now had experience behind them. They knew how to keep the attention and loyalty of their membership. From their earliest days they had always used the "donkey and the carrot" trick. The end of the system and the reward for all loyal members had always been just a few years ahead. Each time the due date arrived, it would be moved on a little.

Throughout the 1960's the anticipation slowly built to a crescendo. Armageddon was due at any time but for some years now no date had been given. The Society had learned from past mistakes not to be too specific. It had adopted a way of using innuendo and then leaving the rest to the over-excited imagination of the membership.

Then in 1966 the new book, *Life Everlasting in Freedom of the Sons of God* suggested a new date for Armageddon. Complete with charts, the Society claimed they were able to work out when the first man Adam was created. Working from this date they counted forward to produce another specific date. They declared :

According to this trustworthy Bible chronology 6,000 years from man's creation will end in 1975, and the seventh period of a thousand years of human history will begin in the fall of 1975 CE ... it would not be by mere chance or accident but would be according to the loving purpose of Jehovah God for the reign of Jesus Christ, the "Lord of the Sabbath," to run parallel with the seventh millennium of man's existence.   PAGES 29,30

The Watchtower and *Awake!* magazines continued to fan the flames of expectation :

The immediate future is certain to be filled with climactic events, for this old system is nearing its complete end. Within a few years at most the final part of Bible prophecy relative to these "last days" will undergo fulfillment, resulting in the liberation of surviving mankind into Christ's 1,000-year reign. What difficult days, but at the same time, what grand days are just ahead.

THE WATCHTOWER 1.5.1968 – PAGE 272

The fact that fifty-four years of the period called the "last days" have already gone by is highly significant. It means that only a few years at most, remain before the corrupt system of things dominating the earth is destroyed by God.

AWAKE! – 8 OCTOBER 1968 – PAGE 13

The Society were to later claim that they never actually said 1975 would bring the end of the system. True, it was only suggested. The Witnesses around the world arrived at the idea that 1975 would be the year, all by themselves! Naturally the Society did not discourage the excitement that swept through the movement. Far be it for the Society to tell its members what to think.

The fervour that followed had to be experienced to be believed. At a series of conventions around the world in the summer of 1968 a new book was introduced, *The Truth that Leads to Eternal Life*. It has since sold over one hundred million copies.

I sat transfixed in the London assembly at Twickenham Stadium, as the speaker explained the reason for the book's release. This small book had been designed so that a weekly study of just one hour covering one chapter a week would complete the book in six months. All other Society books used in Bible studies with interested people were to be put aside.

This was now the book to use. If those we studied with did not show definite signs of getting baptised after six months we were to forget them and move on. Why? Because time was running out – so many people to save and so little time! We were told that the end was now so close that there was no time to waste.

The atmosphere was electrified. The inspired talks that followed brought the stadium to its feet in unanimous applause. Men fought to hold back tears. We were on the brink of entering "The New World." These wonderful men who, we believed, had direct communication with Jehovah God himself, were standing there before us and assuring us that all we had hoped and prayed for was almost here. I can honestly say that I have never experienced such euphoria before and I doubt I ever will again.

I was thirteen years old at the time and longed to leave school and save as many lives as I could by entering the pioneer service.

The Watchtower magazines that followed kept up the excitement. The speakers in the Kingdom Halls were less cautious with their words than those the Society set to print.

Elders announced that they were selling their homes to go pioneering. Many gave up their jobs to join the crusade. Such heroism was actively encouraged by the Society and such men and women were held up as fine examples. Those who were less brave felt guilty – they were too fond of the things of this world.

In the few years that followed there was a certain magic in the air. The brothers and sisters could sense the nearness of all they had hoped for. We did not worry about trivial matters such as how much money we were making, how our careers were progressing, or what type of house we lived in. All that mattered was studying with new people and sharing our joy while there was still time – Time – Time! So much time passed and 1975 came and went, along with many disillusioned Witnesses.

Disappointed Again

The build-up to this date and the tremendous effort to get people into the organization before it was too late had swelled the numbers enormously. Though many had left, the number remaining was still greater than before this build up. Those remaining had proved they would stay despite disappointment.

The Society explained that this was part of the harvesting process and the best had remained and been refined. I stayed. After all we were still told that Armageddon was "just around the corner." At that time I had never studied any of the Society's history independently but had relied on such in house publications as *Jehovah's Witnesses in the Divine Purpose*.

I had by this time left home and started to think for myself a little. I began to question certain anomalies in the movement and was advised that I was developing a "spirit of independence." I expected everything to add up and make sense, after all this was "the Truth" – wasn't it? One senior brother of fifty years standing explained that the most important thing in the congregation was unity. It did not matter so much whether what we believed was accurate so long as we all believed the same. This did nothing to ease the nagging feeling I had, that the Emperor wore no clothes.

Anticipating the disappointment that many brothers and sisters would experience, the Society attempted to place the responsibility for this expectation on the membership by drawing a comparison with the disappointment experienced in 1925 :

> 1925 was a sad year for many of the brothers. Some of them were stumbled; their hopes were dashed. They had hoped to see some of the 'ancient worthies' (men of old like Abraham) resurrected. Instead of it's being considered a 'probability', they read into it that it was a 'certainty' and some prepared for their own loved ones with expectancy of the resurrection.
>
> *1975 YEARBOOK OF JEHOVAH'S WITNESSES* – PAGE – 146

Apparently the disappointed members had

"read into it that it was a certainty."

How else does one understand the statements made by the Society's president in the 1920 booklet, *Millions Now Living Will Never Die?*

> As we have heretofore stated, the great jubilee cycle is due to begin in 1925.

> Therefore we may confidently expect that 1925 will mark the return of Abraham, Isaac, Jacob and the faithful prophets of old, particularly those named by the Apostle in Hebrews chapter eleven, to the condition of human perfection.

> Then, based upon the promises set forth in the divine Word, we must reach the positive and indisputable conclusion that millions now living will never die.

With so many failed prophecies behind them and the biblical warning about false prophets, one would think it appropriate for the Society to lay low for a while. Perhaps even admitting that they had got a little carried away in presuming to be God's prophet.

They could have explained that though they had done their best, they realized that they had let down those who looked to them for guidance. Perhaps an apology to those who had been thrown out for daring to question what time had proved to be false teachings. Of course this would take humility, a quality Christians claim to have. What I am suggesting is summed up in the Society's own words under the heading "Why admit it when you are wrong" :

> Especially does it seem difficult for those in positions of responsibility to admit being wrong. Why? No doubt in many instances this is due to pride. They are concerned with what others may think: they want to "save face," as the saying goes. But, then again, failure to admit being wrong may well be due to feelings of insecurity. A person may feel that his position is threatened if he admits a mistake.
>
> Honesty and empathy also enter the picture. If certain persons are entitled to know that we have erred, we should be willing to admit the wrong. Especially should empathy move us to admit it if another person would otherwise be blamed and suffer for our mistake.   THE WATCHTOWER – 1 SEPTEMBER 1982 – PAGE 28

Despite this advice to their members the Society decided not to admit that they had been wrong. The closest they ever came to an apology was this statement issued through *The Watchtower* magazine in 1980 :

> In modern times such eagerness, commendable in itself, has led to attempts at setting dates for the desired liberation from the suffering and troubles that are the lot of persons throughout the earth. With the appearance of the book *Life Everlasting in Freedom of the Sons of God*, and its comments as to how appropriate it would be for the millennial reign of Christ to parallel the seventh millennium of man's existence, considerable expectation was aroused regarding the year 1975. There were statements made then, and thereafter, stressing that this was only a possibility. Unfortunately, however, along with such cautionary information, there were other statements published that implied that such realization of hopes by that year was more of a probability than a mere possibility. It is to be regretted that these latter statements

apparently overshadowed the cautionary ones and contributed to a build-up of the expectation already initiated.

The Watchtower, commenting on the inadvisability of setting our sights on a certain date, stated :

> If anyone has been disappointed through not following this line of thought, he should now concentrate on adjusting his viewpoint, seeing that it was not the word of God that failed or deceived him and brought disappointment, but that his own understanding was based on **wrong premises**.　　15 JULY, 1976

> **In saying "anyone," *The Watchtower* included all disappointed ones of Jehovah's Witnesses, hence including persons having to do with the publication of the information that contributed to the build-up of hopes centered on that date.**
> THE WATCHTOWER – 15 MARCH 1980 – PAGE 16 (BOLD TYPE ADDED)

These persons having to do with the publication of this information were none other than members of the Governing Body of the Society. They are the same people who claim to be spirit-appointed by God and responsible for providing spiritual food at the proper time, to those they claim to communicate with on God's behalf. Were they now saying that they had only been guessing, and the "wrong premises" that members had based their hopes on was them?

Is this really the same group of men who had referred to themselves as God's prophet as recently as 1972 in an article entitled "Identifying the Prophet?"

> These questions can be answered in the affirmative. Who is the prophet? – However, Jehovah did not let the people of Christendom, as led by the clergy, go without being warned that the League was a counterfeit substitute for the real Kingdom of God. He had a "prophet" to warn them. This "prophet" was not one man, but a body of men and women. It was a small group of footstep followers of Jesus Christ, known then at that time as International Bible Students. Today they are known as Jehovah's Christian Witnesses. They are still proclaiming a warning, and

they have been joined and assisted in their commissioned work by hundreds of thousands of persons who have listened to their message with belief."

Of course it is easy to say that this group act as a prophet of God. It is another thing to prove it. The only way that this can be done is to review the record. What does it show?

THE WATCHTOWER – 1 APRIL 1972 – PAGE 197

Reading this quote brought to mind the scriptural warning made by Jesus in his sermon on the mount :

Beware of false prophets, men who come to you dressed up as sheep while underneath they are savage wolves. You will recognise them by the fruits they bear.   MATTHEW 7:15,16 – NE

Whether this scripture can be applied to the Watchtower Society depends on what kind of fruit they have produced. Have the prophecies made by them ripened or turned bad? Have those that received the Society's fruit been satisfied or disappointed?

The Watchtower Society state that, thousands of people have listened to their message with belief. In view of their record of failed prophecies, do these same people still listen with belief? Those who listened with belief and helped to proclaim the warning were threatened with excommunication if they ever dared to question the Society's "truth" which they have referred to as an "unquestionable certainty".

The Watchtower magazine will often contain articles written by members who have given a lifetime of service and recount what a wonderful experience it has been. For example a recent article by pioneer Carol Allen, who was raised as a Witness, concluded by saying :

The years have been happy ones, filled with love for Jehovah, for each other, and for friends old and new. The two months we spent in Patterson as Paul (husband) received training was the highlight of our life so far. Observing Jehovah's earthly organization up close reaffirmed a conviction passed on to me as part of my precious spiritual heritage: This is indeed God's organization. What a joy to be even a small part of it!

THE WATCHTOWER – 1 OCTOBER 2000 – PAGE 29

There are many more testimonies like this, so obviously there are many who despite the facts facing them, choose to continue believing that the Society is God's organization. As we continue to examine the Watchtower Society's record, to see what it shows, you will be able form your own opinion as to whether they are God's prophet and his exclusive channel of communication with mankind.

This Generation

As Jesus was said to have begun his Kingdom reign in 1914, how much longer could the New World be in coming? The hopes of the Jehovah's Witnesses still hung on one verse of scripture.

Jesus was asked by his disciples when the fall of Jerusalem and the destruction of their temple would be. He gave a detailed description of the events leading up to this. Most Bible students agree that some parts of this prophecy have a greater fulfillment:

> "I tell you this: this present generation will live to see it all."(NE) or "Truly I say to you that this generation will by no means pass away until all things occur." (NWT - MATTHEW 24:34)

Christians have always understood this to be a reference to the generation then living, which was to see the Jewish temple destroyed. It was a repetition of what had been said earlier in Matthew 23:36. Having condemned the Scribes and Pharisees for their hypocrisy and treatment of the prophets, Jesus went on to speak of the destruction of Jerusalem. He was talking to the Scribes and Pharisees and telling them that they would pay for the wrong they had done with their lives.

He then left them and was approached by his disciples who asked him to look at the temple buildings with them. Jesus then repeated his statement concerning the generation then living to his disciples. True to his word, the temple was destroyed 39 years later, and the Scribes and Pharisees with it, within the lifetime of the generation that had been warned.

The Society almost never quoted from the first occasion because the context shows the true meaning of the statement.

They quoted from the second occasion and claimed that Jesus was referring to the generation that would be alive in 1914 when he is said to have begun his reign.

The Watchtower Society has repeated its claim that "the end" would come within the life of that generation, so many times, in so much literature, over so long, that to list all the quotes and revisions of exactly how long a generation is would double the size of this book, which I have deliberately kept brief. This would be both tedious and unnecessary. As with other quotes in this book I have selected only a few from among many to avoid too much repetition.

As this promise, based on what has come to be known as "the 1914 generation," has spanned so many decades, and been the cornerstone of Witness thinking for so long, I have listed a number of these quotes, but have not dissected and explained them as their relevance is self evident. Please note the dates of these quotes and the period of time they cover :

> The thirty-six intervening years since 1914, instead of postponing Armageddon, have only made it closer than most people think. Do not forget: "this generation shall not pass, till all these things be fulfilled." *THE WATCHTOWER* – 1 NOVEMBER 1950 – PAGE 419

> We then are that Generation that will not pass away until there is fulfilled that "great tribulation" such has not occurred since the world's beginning until now, no, nor will occur again. *THE WATCHTOWER* – 15 APRIL 1961 – PAGE 236

> Which generation did Jesus mean? He meant the generation of people who were living in 1914. Those persons yet remaining of that generation are now very old. However, some of them will still be alive to see the end of this wicked system. So of this we can be certain: Shortly now there will be a sudden end to all wickedness and wicked people at Armageddon. Some of the generation living in 1914 will see the end of the system of things and survive it. *YOU CAN LIVE FOREVER IN PARADISE ON EARTH* – PAGE 154

The generation that was old enough to view those events with understanding in 1914 is no longer young. It no longer has many years to run. Already many of its members have died. But Jesus showed us that there would still be members of "this generation" alive at the time of the passing away of this wicked system in both heaven and earth.

THE WATCHTOWER – 1 MAY 1967 – PAGE 262

Jesus was obviously speaking about those who were old enough to witness with understanding what took place when the "last day" began. Jesus was saying that some of those persons who were alive at the appearance of the "sign of the last days" would be alive when God bought this system to an end.

Even if we presume that youngsters 15 years of age would be perceptive enough to realize the import of what happened in 1914, it would still make the youngest of "this generation" nearly 70 years old today. So the great majority of the generation to which Jesus was referring has already passed away in death. The remaining ones are approaching old age. And remember, Jesus said that the end of this wicked world would come before that generation passed away in death. This, of itself, tells us that the years left before the foretold end comes cannot be many.   AWAKE! – 8 OCTOBER 1968 – PAGES 13,14

But there are people still living who were alive in 1914 and saw what was happening then who were old enough that they still remember those events. This generation is getting up in years now. A great number of them have already passed away in death ... This means that only a short time is left before the end comes.   THE TRUTH THAT LEADS TO ETERNAL LIFE PAGE 95 – 1968

From a purely human point of view, it could appear that these developments could hardly take place before the generation of 1914 disappears from the scene. But the fulfillment of all the foretold events affecting the generation of 1914 does not depend on comparatively slow human action. Jehovah's prophetic word through Christ Jesus is: "This generation (of 1914) will by no means pass away until all things occur." (Luke 21:32) And Jehovah, who is the source of inspired and unfailing prophecy, will bring the fulfilment of his son's words in a relatively short time.   THE WATCHTOWER – 15 MAY 1984 – PAGE 6

Just as Jesus' prophecies regarding Jerusalem were fulfilled within the life span of the generation of the year 33 CE, so his prophecies regarding 'the time of the end' will be fulfilled within the life span of the generation of 1914. Yes, you may live to see this promised New Order, along with the survivors of the generation of 1914, the generation that will not pass away.

THE WATCHTOWER – 15 MAY 1984 – PAGES 6-7

Most important, this magazine builds confidence in the creator's promise of a peaceful and secure world before the generation that saw the events of 1914 CE passes away.

AWAKE! MAGAZINE, PART OF MASTHEAD 1982 – 1995

Most important, this magazine builds confidence in the creator's promise of a peaceful and secure new world that is about to replace the present wicked, and lawless system of things.

AWAKE! MAGAZINE, PART OF MASTHEAD FROM 1995

These few quotes are sufficient to show that, according to the Watchtower Society, the promised New World and of course the mass destruction of most of the people on earth would come before the 1914 generation passed away. The Bible states that the normal life expectancy of a human is seventy years. (Psalms 90:10)

Why did not the Society just alter their understanding of this verse as they have with many others? Could it be that this verse of scripture had been used as the carrot for too long? How many times could the Jehovah's Witnesses be disappointed and still continue? Raymond Franz who was a member of the Society's elite Governing Body until resigning in 1980 wrote the following words in 1989. More about his stand for truth can be found in the next chapter :

What especially distinguishes their teachings from any other denomination is the keystone doctrine centred on 1914 as the date when Christ's active rulership began, his commencing judgement then and, above all, his selecting the Watchtower organization as his official channel, his assigning full control of all his earthly interests to a "faithful and discreet slave class" and, factually, giving ultimate authority to its ruling body. Any abandoning of that keystone teaching would affect the whole doctrinal structure and is extremely unlikely, and would be very difficult to explain. There is no reason at present to expect other than a determined effort through the columns of the Watchtower and other publications to shore up their defence of the interpretations supporting that date or resulting from it, and to sustain faith in the claims based on it. Most important among those claims is that related to an organizational authority, and here again there is presently a very intensive campaign to solidify support of, and loyalty to, that authority structure.

CRISIS OF CONSCIENCE – RAYMOND FRANZ – PAGE 337

How long would it be before the Society were forced by the passage of time, to admit that they had been wrong for a hundred years? Many were wondering how much longer "this generation" could last. The Society were aware of this and went out of their way to insist that the reward would come within the lifetime of those who witnessed World War I. They knew that they could sustain the loss of members such a turn-around could bring far better if they built up the numbers of followers first. Besides, many who were joining were young and could afford to wait if the carrot moved on again. Those who were too old would probably stay as well. After a lifetime of conditioning and reliance on the Society, they would find it hard to cope on the outside without the continual guidance they now depended on. In 1988 I wrote :

Within a few years the Society will drop the bombshell. The membership will be told that this is a test of faith. They will be asked whether they were only selfishly serving with a date in view, or whether they really love Jehovah. It will be presented as a wonderful opportunity to use the extension of time to save more lives by getting more people into the organization. They will be told that God himself has lovingly held back the destruction so that more people can come to know about salvation through the Watchtower Society. How do I know this? – Because history repeats itself. Great as the shock waves will be, the Society will survive, they have played this game before.

9

ALL EAGER FOR THE TREAT

1990 to 2000 – and Beyond

The march of time moved on relentlessly. The Watchtower Society began to alter their definition of "a generation" and stretch their credulity to the limit. When 1995 arrived they realized they would have to come clean and admit that they were wrong. That Armageddon was in fact further away than they had thought, unless there was another way out.

Realising that time was running out, the Society's then President Fred Franz, referring to the promised new world declared :

> But we are as strong for it as we ever were, and we are appreciating it all the more the longer we have to wait for it. It is something worth waiting for, even if it required a million years.
>
> THE WATCHTOWER – 15 DECEMBER 1991 – PAGE 11

The faithful men of old had not returned physically as promised. The promised return of Jesus to earth had been explained away as an invisible return that they had failed to notice. It was now claimed that many of the promises regarding Israel had been fulfilled on the Witnesses in a spiritual or pictorial way. The promised paradise was, for now, a spiritual paradise.

It would have only been one step more for the Society to declare that Armageddon was to be fought in a spiritual realm and would be one more invisible fulfilment not seen by the members. They could have written another book explaining that Armageddon had already taken place invisibly and they had missed this event too, but could explain it all, using that wonderful tool of hindsight. Perhaps giving the due apology for having encouraged some of the older members to spend their lives speculating about how many days or years make up a generation. Instead they said :

> Eager to see the end of this evil system, Jehovah's people have at times speculated about the time when the "great tribulation" would break out, even tying this to calculations of what is the lifetime of a generation since 1914. However we "bring a heart of wisdom in." Not by speculating about how many days or years make up a generation, but by thinking about how we "count our days" in bringing joyful praise to Jehovah. (Psalm 90:12) Rather than provide a rule for measuring time, the term "generation" as used by Jesus refers principally to contemporary people of a certain historic period, with their identifying characteristics.
>
> Is anything to be gained, then, by looking for dates or by speculating about the literal lifetime of a "generation"? Far from it! Therefore, in the final fulfilment of Jesus' prophecy today, "this generation" apparently refers to the people of the earth who see the sign of Christ's presence but fail to mend their ways. Does our more precise viewpoint on "this Generation" mean that Armageddon is further away than we had thought? Not at all.
>
> THE WATCHTOWER – 1 NOVEMBER 1995 – PAGES 17,19,20

Did you notice that the Society did not say – We have at times speculated, but **"Jehovah's people have at times speculated."** The blame for a lifetime of misinterpreting the scriptures and making false prophecies in God's name is shared with the membership. These are the same members that were threatened with excommunication if they ever dared to challenge the pronouncements coming from the Society, who claim to be "God's mouthpiece."

Having spent the last hundred years warning their members and millions of non-members that the world as we know it is about to end, the Society eventually admits that the single verse of scripture that they have based this prediction on is now to be understood differently. Surely this means that Armageddon is further away than they had thought? According to the Watchtower Society **"Not at all!"**

Is this an honest way to deal with such a fundamental shift of belief?

Many of the membership had built their lives around the timescale dictated to them by the Society. Some had not planned for retirement having been categorically assured that they would never reach old age. Others had sacrificed their careers and family life to give greater service. What now?

The Society is fond of assuring its members that God will one day reward them for the sacrifices they have made. They quote from the Bible "for God is not unrighteous so as to forget your work and the love you showed for his name." (Hebrews 6:10) Is it showing love for someone's name to spread false promises in their name and make it an object of ridicule?

What of the members who secretly doubted the Society's advice and went to college and later took up a full time career? Some even married and had families while feeling guilty for totally ignoring the Society's advice. Such people at the time were considered "weak in the faith," and yet a lifetime later their decisions have proved to be based on a more accurate view of the future than the Society had proclaimed. They did show a lack of faith in the Watchtower Society, but then the Bible states that the requirement for Christians is faith in Jesus Christ.

As Witnesses are regularly told not to serve with a date in mind, one could ask whether these failed prophecies matter that much to the membership? The real difficulty facing Jehovah's Witnesses today is not the challenge of picking themselves up, dusting themselves off, and starting all over again. It is whether they are unanimous in the belief that their God is really directing the Watchtower Society.

After more than a century of false prophecy and broken promises it is clear that someone has got it all dreadfully wrong. Either the Watchtower Society does have the world's only special line of communication with God, or they have been guessing.

Have they proved themselves to be "faithful and discreet?" In their own words sighted earlier :

> Of course, it is easy to say that this group acts as a prophet of God. It is another thing to prove it. The only way that this can be done is to review the record. What does it show?
>
> THE WATCHTOWER – 1 APRIL 1992 – PAGE 197

Over the last few years there has been a subtle conditioning of the membership to accept changed teachings. Articles have appeared playing down the importance of how far away the end of the present world system is. Long explanations as to why truth is slowly revealed through God's mouthpiece and how this slowness involves changing previously held "truths." The following quotes are taken from the Watchtower article "O God, Send out your Light":

> Jehovah is very considerate in the way he makes his purpose known to his servants. Instead of revealing the truth all at once in one blinding flash of light, he enlightens us progressively. Our trek along life's pathway might be compared to a walk that a hiker takes...as the sun continues its ascent, he can see further and further into the distance. So it is with the spiritual light God provides. He allows us to discern a few things at a time.

> Just as the apostles understood many prophecies concerning the Messiah only after Jesus' resurrection, Christians today understand Bible prophecy in its finest detail only after it has been fulfilled.

> A brilliant flash of light on one Bible subject sometimes leads God's anointed servants, "the faithful and discreet slave," to re-examine related topics.
>
> THE WATCHTOWER – 15 MARCH 2000 – PAGES 10,11,13

When a group of self appointed spiritual leaders make so many errors, the obvious question is; how many other scriptures have they misused and why, if they really are guided by God? Would it not be better to have no explanation for certain Bible passages, than to spread misleading teachings? If someone asks for directions, is it not better to decline rather than send them the wrong way. Having been misled so often, many more members are now realizing that the search for truth is a personal responsibility. For those who have already spent their lives waiting for Armageddon and a promised "new world," it is easier to ignore all the facts and continue to imagine that the Emperor still wears a fine suit of clothes.

The reason for dwelling on chronology and dates is that, as mentioned before, the Society has had an obsession with time since its earliest days. Before moving on, let's take a brief look at why dates are so important to the belief structure of the Watchtower Society. Later on, we can examine other aspects of the Witnesses beliefs.

Jerusalem and 607 BCE*

One of the most important dates upon which the Watchtower Society build their own dating system is 607 BCE. This is the date that Pastor Russell originally claimed Jerusalem was destroyed. The Society has never changed their mind on the accuracy of this inherited date.

It is by counting from 607 BCE as the beginning of the Gentile times that they arrive at 1914. They calculate the reference in Daniel 4:16 of "seven times" to be seven lots of 360, the number of days in a Jewish year. This comes to 2,520 years. Counting from 607 BCE the date 1914 is arrived at. If 607 BCE is not the starting point, then the date 1914 is of no significance.

All other important dates in which the Society claims to have featured as a fulfilment of prophecy are calculated by working from 1914. The "three and a half years" are added to arrive at 1918, when they say the spirit of God entered into them and revived their work, appointing them as the "faithful and discreet slave." This was also the year the chosen ones were resurrected to heaven.

We could just take the Society's word for it that Jerusalem fell in 607 BCE. Then again, given their record with dates, I think it would be sensible to check. Listed below are a few of the numerous references to Jerusalem's fall :

■ The final destruction of the city (Jerusalem) was in … 586 BCE
  LIGHT FROM THE ANCIENT PAST – JACK FINNEGAN – PAGE 223

*BCE – Before the Common Era.

- Nebuchadnezzar ... destroyed Jerusalem ... in 586 BCE

  THE ENCYCLOPAEDIA AMERICANA – VOLUME 16 PAGE 31

- Finally, in the year 586 BCE Jerusalem itself was taken.

  THE STORY OF ANCIENT NATIONS – W.L. WESTERMAN – PAGE 69

- On the 7th day of the fifth month 586 BCE Jerusalem was destroyed. ENCYCLOPAEDIA BRITANNICA – VOLUME 15 – PAGE 383

- Jerusalem fell in 586 BCE.

  YALE ORIENTAL SERIES RESEARCHES – VOL. XV

- In July 586 BCE ... a breach was made in the wall of Jerusalem.

  HISTORY OF THE HEBREWS – F.K. SAUNDERS

Any encyclopaedia can be checked for further confirmation.

As it is clear that the real date for Jerusalem's fall is 586 BCE and not 607 BCE, all the other important Watchtower dates are without foundation. A rumour of this nature existed when I was a Witness and I had been to the library and checked every reference book available and confirmed that this was one more false date to add to the list.

My attempts to square the sum with elders, who I felt I could approach privately, were met with strongly worded advice. In a nutshell, I was told to drop it or suffer the consequences. It was on one such occasion that the principle of unity being more important than truth was explained to me.

A Crisis of Conscience

In 1965 Raymond Franz, the nephew of the Society's then President, was appointed as part of a five man team to help carry out research for the compilation of the Society's Bible encyclopaedia, *Aid to Bible Understanding*. This sincere man spent five years working on this assignment, and was during this time appointed as a member of the Governing Body. In 1980 he was to leave the Society and write a book called *Crisis of Conscience*. The following quotation is taken from this book :

Months of research were spent on this one subject of "Chronology" and it resulted in the longest article in the "Aid" publication.

Much of the time was spent endeavouring to find some proof, some backing in history, for the 607 BCE date so crucial to our calculation for 1914. Charles Ploeger, a member of the headquarters staff, was at that time serving as a secretary for me and he searched through the libraries of the New York City area for anything that might substantiate that date historically.

We found absolutely nothing in support of 607 BCE. All historians pointed to a date twenty years later... Everything pointed to a date twenty years shorter than our published chronology claimed.

Though I found this disquieting, I wanted to believe that our chronology was right in spite of all the contrary evidence that such evidence was somehow in error. Thus, in preparing the material for the "Aid" book, much of the time and space was spent in trying to weaken the credibility of the archeological and historical evidence that would make erroneous our 607 BCE date and give a different starting point for our calculations and therefore an ending date different from 1914.

PAGES 28 & 29 (US SPELLING)

Despite knowing this, the Society continued to mislead its membership rather than admit that none of its sums added up and went ahead with the Book *Aid to Bible Understanding*.

The Society can withstand considerable turbulence among its followers and still weather the storm, but how much discord can it cope with among its chosen few behind the closed doors of its head office in New York? Over the last hundred years there have been a number of problems at this level. As we have seen, the policy in 1917 was to dismiss anyone who would not show unquestioning obedience. This way of handling problems has been maintained to this day and was used to cover up the scandal that erupted in 1980.

Raymond Franz was a third generation Witness who had been a Witness for all of his 60 years, most of them working directly for the Society at the highest organizational level. For nine of those years he was a member of the Governing Body. He had proved himself to be a totally dedicated and loyal servant, serving for many years as a foreign missionary.

It came to the Society's notice that a growing number of

members were concerned about the validity of some of the Society's key teachings, when measured against the plain teachings of the Bible.

There was concern over the Society teaching that Christ is only a mediator for the 144,000 chosen ones, who hope to live in heaven, and not the ordinary members. Doubts were voiced about the idea that there were two classes with different hopes, in view of the Bible's clear teaching that all who profess faith in Christ will join him in heaven. Questions were asked about the Society's teaching that all faithful men of old will not go to heaven, even though the Bible plainly states that they will. These and other long held Watchtower Society beliefs were privately discussed among many long serving members, mostly pioneers.

There followed a witch-hunt in which many dozens of sincere Bible students were disfellowshipped on the charge of apostasy against the Society. Raymond Franz, the nephew of Frank Franz, then president of the Watchtower Society, was forced to resign from the Governing Body over doubts about his unquestioning obedience to the organization, and left the headquarters in New York to live in a trailer home and start over again.

Further doubts regarding the Society's claim to be the only way to salvation, and their view of Jesus Christ, led to many others being forced out. This was the biggest shake up in many years, yet amazingly most of the membership is unaware of these events.

These men and women are witnesses in the true sense of the word. They have given the best years of their lives to a calling, believing that it was "the truth." They served at the highest level in the Society. They have already proved that they are seekers of truth. When they realized that their beliefs did not amount to "the truth," they spoke out as

WITNESSES TO TRUTH,
regardless of the personal cost.

Raymond Franz, as part of the Governing Body, was responsible for writing some of the literature supplied to the membership. He was believed when he was part of the Society. His testimony is worth no less now that he has found the courage to leave and speak out.

His fascinating story along with copies of the correspondence that took place is available in his book. For an in-depth insight into the inner workings of the Watchtower Society and photocopies of their history of pronouncements, I can recommend *Crisis of Conscience*, a heavyweight textbook by Raymond Franz. (Commentary Press – Atlanta – Released in 1983, revised and updated in 1999 available through Amazon Books).

Many of those whose conscience also moved them to speak out and leave had served as Witnesses for many decades, in some cases more than forty years. The following quote is taken from a chapter in the book just highlighted, entitled "Price of Conscience" :

> They include persons who were prominent members of the Witnesses' international headquarters staff at Brooklyn, New York; men who were travelling superintendents and elders; women who spent long years in missionary and evangelistic work. When they first became Witnesses, they had often cut off all previous friendships with persons of other faiths, since such associations are discouraged among Jehovah's Witnesses. For the rest of their life their only friends have been among those of their faith. Some had built their whole life plans around the goals set before them by the organization, letting these control the amount of education they sought, the type of work they did, their decisions as to marriage, and whether they had children or remained childless. Their "investment" was a large one, involving some of life's most precious assets. And now they have seen all of this disappear, wiped out in a matter of a few hours.   PAGE 4

Among those that left the Bethel home was Randy Watters, who went on to establish a Christian help group for the many thousands of Witnesses that decided truth lay elsewhere. The help group known as "Bethel Ministries", now called "Free Minds", has helped many of these sincere people examine the Watchtower Society in detail. They have had to come to terms with the shock of finding that they could no longer support an organization that has failed the very test that it set for others.

To dismiss such dedicated long serving members because of their desire to speak the truth is a serious indictment. To label them as evil slaves and erase them from memory may have

97

worked in the past, but as their numbers increase and more find the courage to speak out with documented reasons for their discontent, they will eventually get their message across to the many Witnesses who have never questioned.

Is Sincerity Enough?

Does the Bible say that God rejects Christians if their understanding of certain scriptures is wrong, however sincere they are? Christians believe that faith in Jesus is the requirement for life, and that all human mistakes and failings can be forgiven if forgiveness is asked for :

> If thou, LORD, should keep account of sins, who, O Lord, could hold up his head? But in thee is forgiveness, and therefore thou art revered. PSALMS 130:3,4 – NE

> He that hears my word and believes him that sent me has everlasting life, and he does not come into judgment but has passed over from death to life. JOHN 5:24 – NWT

According to the Watchtower Society, more is required. They maintain that in addition to faith in Jehovah through Jesus, Christians must have accurate knowledge.

Accurate Knowledge

The essence of the Watchtower Society's movement has often been explained by them quoting from their own mistranslated version of this scriptural text :

> This means everlasting life, their taking in accurate knowledge of you, the only true God, and of the one whom you sent forth Jesus Christ. JOHN 17:3 – NWT

The play on the words "accurate knowledge" has provided a purpose for the Society's existence and the need for so many explanatory publications. Other Bibles such as the New English state that eternal life is dependent on knowing God and Jesus. The basis for the Society condemning all other Christian movements is to accuse them of failing to dispense accurate knowledge to their adherents.

They have now dropped the word "accurate" from their

translation but still leave the reader with a less than accurate understanding. This taking in of knowledge is said to be so important, that unless one joins their organization and buys their books, they will not gain the knowledge required to gain life.

Inaccurate Knowledge

As accurate knowledge has been made the requirement for salvation, how does this requirement affect the founders of the Watchtower?

Pastor Russell, for example, not only held very different views to the present day Society, but also published them around the world. The book *The Time is at Hand*, which was quoted from earlier sold 2,000,000 copies. This was a huge achievement considering it was published over one hundred years ago. The book contained a vast amount of inaccurate knowledge. Many people left their own churches to follow him. Those churches said that Pastor Russell was teaching a false understanding of the Bible. He condemned these churches for not accepting the light.

If he, or any member of his sect were to return to earth today, they would have to reject many of the "truths" they then believed or be disfellowshipped by the present Society. However this is not how the members are instructed to view their founders. Very few know what beliefs they held. These men are still believed to be part of the chosen few who will go to heaven in place of faithful men of old like Abraham.

What of the sincere Christians who refused to join the Society, or left because they said it was a false prophet? In the Society's eyes, these too will perish at God's hand along with all other religions. They have stipulated that accurate knowledge is the requirement for salvation and insist that it can only be obtained from them. Without it, salvation is not possible however sincere a person may be. Does their record show that they have lived up to their own requirement?

Off With Their Heads!

The prime object of the Society's hatred is Christendom – all other Christian churches. Since their earliest days they have publicly attacked them. They believe that the church leaders are

99

bent on the overthrow of their organization, led by the Devil, and will stop at nothing to achieve this aim. The membership now has a persecution complex against the clergy, who are not just criticised but condemned to death. Christendom is deemed to be past hope of redemption :

> She has been a long time in coming to her day of reckoning. But now at last her sin has found her out, has caught up with her. The end that Jehovah has decreed for her is about to come upon her, and she may expect no mercy from him. She is past all possibility of repenting and converting to him.
>
> THE NATIONS SHALL KNOW THAT I AM JEHOVAH – PAGE 125

The book the above quote is taken from attempts to apply Ezekiel's prophecy concerning Israel to the leaders of Christian churches and all other religions in the world. Ezekiel's warning to Israel is applied in an amazing way. A few of the titles and subtitles are listed below:

> *The days of Christendom are numbered.*
> *Christendom will know – at her end.*
> *Detestable religious things over which to sigh.*
> *Christendom infected with deadly demonism.*
> *Christendom's fiery destruction from the celestial chariot.*
> *Where the smashing of heads begins.*
> *Hypocritical religionists stunned by the news.*

Thousands of verbal and printed attacks have been made on the integrity of religious leaders. The fact is that religious leaders seldom say a word about Jehovah's Witnesses, despite the way the Watchtower Society persecutes and reviles them. If occasionally the Witnesses are criticised, it is in response to their numerous damning attacks made in almost every publication they print. The clergy I have spoken with have great compassion for the Witnesses, feeling they have been misled.

The Society would like its members to believe that they are a persecuted minority who survive only with God's protection. They have gone out of their way to provoke the church leaders. Considering the hostile statements directed at them, the church leaders show considerable restraint. Far from the clergy persecuting the Witnesses the reverse is true.

10

THE WITNESSES' OWN BIBLE

One of the Society's most enduring books is their translation of the Bible. Most members believe that this was translated from the original text in an attempt to provide a more accurate Bible.

All members use this Bible almost exclusively. Most Witnesses say they will use any translation, but in reality, for a member to sit through a meeting with a Bible other than the Society's would be seen as a sign of rebellion. It is unthinkable for a speaker to use a different translation for the duration of a lecture. Occasionally quotes from other Bibles are used if the wording suits the particular point the speaker wishes to make.

For any serious debate, the Society's New World Translation (NWT) is always used. To attempt to use any other translation would lead to counselling being given, as it is seen as a failure to follow the Society's admonition. Why do Jehovah's Witnesses place such importance on their own Bible?

On the whole, the Witnesses' Bible is a fairly reasonable modern translation. Unfortunately though, some of the main teachings of the Bible have been subtly altered to fit in with their beliefs by the alteration or addition of key words. All other Bibles word verses differently but give the same inference. They lead to the same unanimous understanding the writer was trying to convey. The Society's Bible is the odd man out.

Most of these differences are a result of the way Witnesses view Jesus. To them Jesus is an angel, a Son of God, part of creation. A relationship with Jehovah God is essential to gain life.

This is only obtainable by joining their organization. They state :

> But because the increasing flock of Jehovah's Christian Witnesses proclaim his name (Jehovah) everywhere as the name to call upon for salvation through Jesus Christ, more and more people are seeking the life giving association with these Witnesses.
>
> THE NATIONS SHALL KNOW THAT I AM JEHOVAH
> – PAGE 333 – BRACKETS ADDED

They do not accept as stated in the Bible that :

> This Jesus is the stone rejected by the builders which has become the keystone – and you the builders. There is no salvation in anyone else at all, for there is no other name granted to men, by which we may receive salvation.   ACTS 4:11,12 – NE

Witnesses totally reject the teaching of the Trinity as set out in the Nicene Creed in AD 325. In order to dilute the impact that Jesus has, many Bible texts have been altered. There are far too many incidents of this to list them all. Just a few are shown here to illustrate the way in which this has been done.

Speaking of Jesus –

> … and bestowed on him the name over every name.
>
> PHILIPPIANS 2:9 NE

> **… and kindly gave him the name that is above every other name.**   PHILIPPIANS 2:9 – NWT

✳ ✳ ✳

> He is the image of the invisible God; his is the primacy over all created things.   COLOSSIANS 1:15 – NE

> **He is the image of the invisible God, the firstborn of all creation ;**   COLOSSIANS 1:15 – NWT

In the following text the word "other" had been added three times:

> The whole universe has been created through him and for him. And he exists before everything, and all things are held together in him. COLOSSIANS 1:16,17 – NE

> **All other things have been created through him and for him. Also, he is before all other things and by means of him all other things were made to exist.** COLOSSIANS 1:16,17 – NWT

The NWT has added the word " other," to alter the meaning of the text. In subsequent printings, brackets have been put around the added words. This is of little help, particularly when the text is read aloud at "meetings." The word "other" which it is claimed is there to clarify the scripture has no place being there, as an interlinear Bible will show. Here are a few more translations of the same scripture.

> He is the likeness of the unseen God, born first, before all creation – for it was by him that all things were created. MOFFATT

> He was born before creation began. J.B. PHILIPS

> Begotten before all creation. BARCLAYS NEW TRANSLATION

> The firstborn before all creation. BERKLEY VERSION

The same result is achieved in the following texts by using the words "by means of":

> What I mean is, that God was in Christ reconciling the world to himself. CORINTHIANS 5:19 – NE

> **Namely that God was by means of Christ reconciling the world to himself.** 2 CORINTHIANS 5:19 – NWT

✳ ✳ ✳

> All that came to be was alive with his life and that life was the light of men. JOHN 1:4 – NE

> **By means of him was life, and the life was the light of men.** JOHN 1:4 – NWT

Who is the Word?

One of the most debated verses in the Witnesses' Bible is John 1:1, where Jesus is referred to in the Witnesses' Bible as **"a god"** :

> In the beginning was the Word, and the Word was towards the God, and God was the Word.
>
> JOHN 1:1 – *KINGDOM INTERLINEAR*, A WATCHTOWER PUBLICATION

> In the beginning was the Word, and the Word was with God and the Word was God.   JOHN 1:1 – KING JAMES

> When all things began, the Word already was. The Word dwelt with God, and what God was, the Word was.   JOHN 1:1 - NE

> **In the beginning the Word was, and the Word was with God, and the word was a god.**   JOHN 1:1 – NWT

The following quotes are taken from the comments of Greek scholars :

- A shocking mistranslation ... obsolete and incorrect ... it is neither scholarly nor reasonable to translate John 1:1 "the Word was a god."   DR J.R. MANTEY

- A frightful mistranslation ... if the Jehovah's Witnesses take this translation seriously, they are polytheist's.

  DR BRUCE M. METZGER OF PRINCETON

- This anarthrous (used without the article) construction does not mean what the indefinite 'a' means in English. It is monstrous to translate the phrase "the Word was a god."

  DR SAMUEL J. MIKOLASKI OF SWITZERLAND

- The Jehovah's Witness people evidence an abysmal ignorance of the basic tenets of Greek grammar in their mistranslation of John 1:1.   DR PAUL L. KAUFMAN OF OREGON

- I have never heard of, any Greek scholar who would agree to the interpretation of this verse insisted upon by the Jehovah's

Witnesses ... I have never encountered one of them who had any knowledge of the Greek language.

DR JAMES L. BOYER OF INDIANA

■ The deliberate distortion of truth by this sect is seen in their New Testament translation. John 1:1 is translated"... the Word was a god." A translation which is grammatically impossible ... it is abundantly clear that a sect which can translate the New Testament like that is intellectually dishonest.

DR WILLIAM BARCLAY, GLASGOW UNIVERSITY

■ The predicate (God) stands emphatically first as in IV: 24. It is necessarily without the article ... No idea of inferiority of nature is suggested by the form of expression, which simply affirms the true deity of the word ... in the third clause 'the Word' is declared to be 'God' and so included in the deity of the Godhead.

DR B.F. WESTCOTT

■ So numerous and clear are the arguments and testimonies of scriptures in favour of the true deity of Christ, that I can hardly imagine how, on the rules of fair interpretation, this doctrine can by any man be called into doubt. Especially the passage, John 1:1-3 is so clear and so superior to all exception, that by no daring efforts of either commentators or critics, can it be snatched out of the hands of defenders of truth.

DR. J.J. GERISBACH

The Name Over Every Name

In keeping with the Watchtower Society's belief that Jehovah is the name to call on for salvation, they have inserted this name at every opportunity. They claim that all Bibles should bear this name as frequently, but other translators have tried to hide the name. They claim that they alone are upholding the divine name.

On closer examination a different picture emerges. The foreword of their Bible explains that the divine name appears many times in the Hebrew Scriptures, but fails to appear in the Greek text. It has been replaced with "Kyri,os" meaning Lord and "The.os" meaning God. They claim they have been authorised

105

to restore the divine name.

If we accept this explanation, though other scholars disagree with this assumption, we must ask how the Society knows where to replace, for example, the word Lord with Jehovah? They say they do this by always using the name Jehovah when the Greek scripture appears to be a quotation from a Hebrew scripture where the divine name was used. This at first seems reasonable but they have been overzealous and not stuck to this rule.

The original translators were aware that "The Lord" through-out the New Testament referred to Jesus, the exception being where the term "The Lord God" was used. In many instances where the context of the chapter being read makes it clear beyond question that "The Lord" is a reference to Jesus, the Watchtower Society have substituted the word Jehovah. This has made it possible to produce a Bible, which shifts the emphasis away from Jesus as Lord and places the name Jehovah in this position. From the many instances of this I have selected just a few to show how this has been done :

> If on your lips is the confession, 'Jesus is Lord' and in your heart the faith that God raised him from the dead, then you will find salvation ... Scripture says 'Everyone who had faith in him will be saved from shame' – everyone: there is no distinction between Jew and Greek, because the Lord is Lord of all, and is rich enough for the need of all who invoke him. For everyone, as it says again – Everyone who invokes the name of the Lord will be saved.
>
> ROMANS 10:9-13 – NE

> **For if you publicly declare that 'Word in your own mouth,' that 'Jesus is Lord,' and exercise faith in your heart that God raised him from the dead, you will be saved...For the scripture says: " None that rests his faith on him will be disappointed." For there is no distinction between Jew and Greek, for there is the same Lord over all, who is rich to all those calling upon him. For everyone who calls on the name of Jehovah will be saved.**
>
> ROMANS 10:9-13 – NWT

✳ ✳ ✳

If we live, we live for the Lord; and if we die, we die for the Lord. Whether therefore we live or die, we belong to the Lord. This is why Christ died and came to life again, to establish his Lordship over dead and living.   ROMANS 14:8,9 – NE

...for both if we live, we live to Jehovah, and if we die, we die to Jehovah. Therefore both if we live and if we die, we belong to Jehovah. For to this end Christ died and came to life again, that he might be Lord over both the dead and the living.
ROMANS 14:8,9 – NWT

✳ ✳ ✳

My judge is the Lord. So pass no premature judgment; wait until the Lord comes.   1 CORINTHIANS 4:4,5 – NE

...he that examines me is Jehovah. Hence we do not judge anything before the due time, until the Lord comes.
1 CORINTHIANS 4:4,5 – NWT

In the verse below the name "Jehovah" is used again. Throughout this chapter the Apostle Paul is talking of the Lord's evening meal. He quotes the words of Jesus and refers to him as Lord Jesus. In the preceding eight verses Jesus is referred to as Lord five times. Why is the Lord rendered as Jehovah in verse 32? Reading any other Bible the whole chapter makes sense and the idea of adding the divine name is deliberately misleading.

"However when we are judged
we are disciplined by Jehovah."
1 CORINTHIANS 11:32 – NWT

To the Israelites, which included Jews, the Lord was Jehovah. They were still looking to him for salvation through the law covenant. Paul was trying to show them that the Lord was now addressed by the name Jesus. This was The Sacred Secret. Until then Israelites believed that they could gain salvation by calling on Jehovah. The Christian belief was that now both Jews and Greeks, in fact "everyone" who calls on the name of Jesus could be saved. The Witnesses have stumbled on this. They say they recognize Jesus as Lord, but where the word Lord appears in the

Bible, wherever possible they change it for the name Jehovah.
This was the mistake the Jews were making at the very time.
Talking of Israel's lack of faith in Jesus, Paul went on to say :

> They stumbled over the 'stumbling stone' mentioned in scrip-
> ture: here I am laying in Zion a stumbling stone a rock to trip
> them up; but he who has faith in him will not be put to shame.
>
> ROMANS 9:32,33 – NE

The Witnesses have stumbled on this. The Witnesses believe
that Jesus is the rock mass but fail to realize that they are par-
tially rejecting him. Paul says that it is faith in Jesus' name that
is the requirement for Christians. The Witnesses say works of
faith in Jehovah's name are needed. It is this issue that separates
the Jehovah's Witnesses from all other Christian sects. It is their
claim that this further proves that they alone are the only true
Christian movement on earth today. The following scripture,
though obviously not written with Witnesses in mind, does
sum up their position.

> Brothers, my deepest desire and my prayer to God is for their
> salvation. To their zeal for God I can testify; but it is an ill-
> informed zeal. For they ignore God's way of righteousness, and
> try to set up their own, and therefore they have not submitted
> themselves to God's righteousness. For Christ ends the law and
> brings righteousness for everyone who has faith.
>
> ROMANS 10: 1-3 – NE

The Witnesses have been led to believe that belonging to a
Society, which claims to be Israel restored – a new nation, is the
way to righteousness, that calling on the name of Jehovah, just
as the original nation did, is the way to salvation. They can
show this in their Bible. Can they show it in any other bible?

The following quotes show how other alterations have been
made to rob Jesus of his Divinity :

> For it is in Christ that the complete being of the godhead dwells
> embodied, and in him you have been brought to completion.
>
> COLOSSIANS 2:9,10 – NE

> **...because it is in him that all the fullness of the divine quality
> dwells bodily.** COLOSSIANS 2:9,10 – NWT

✳ ✳ ✳

God answered, 'I am; that is who I AM. Tell them I AM has sent
you to them'   EXODUS 3:14 – NE

**At this God said to Moses "I SHALL PROVE TO BE WHAT I
SHALL PROVE TO BE."**   EXODUS 3:14 – NWT

✳ ✳ ✳

Jesus said, "In very truth I tell you, before Abraham was born, I
AM."   JOHN 8:58 – NE

**Jesus said to them, "Most truly I say to you, before Abraham
came into existence, I have been."**   JOHN 8:58 – NWT

In Exodus, I AM has been replaced with I SHALL PROVE TO
BE, and in John with I HAVE BEEN. Jesus is quoting from the
Hebrew Scriptures, and an interlinear Bible will show that Jesus
used the Greek 'EGO EIMI.' This is present tense and is always
translated as I AM. According to Greek scholars there is no
exception. For Witnesses to accept that Jesus has always been
would mean that other Christians are correct to believe he is not
part of creation.

To fully grasp the import of the alterations in these texts, it is
necessary to read the complete texts in your own Bible and
compare them to the New World Translation.

Prove These Things for Yourselves

Jehovah's Witnesses are told by their Society that their Bible is
the most accurate translation in the world. The members accept
this as fact. They dismiss out of hand any suggestion that their
Bible had been altered to support their own beliefs. The search
for truth is not aided by such treatment of Scripture. Before anyone can decide whether or not they believe Christian theology,
it is necessary for them to read an accurate rendering of the
Bible-writers intended meaning.

These few examples show that a seeker of truth will come to
a different conclusion by reading the Witnesses' Bible. To the
Witnesses this is further proof that they alone have the only

accurate Bible. They claim that, though other Bibles give an idea of what is required of Christians, only their Bible will fully convey the right understanding.

Many terms used in the organization which are said to be Bible-based, are only found in their own translation. These "theocratic terms" appear strange to readers of other translations.

You may choose to believe that the Watchtower Society is correct to render the verses the way they do and that all other Bibles are wrong! What is important is that the conclusions you come to are based on your own independent study. The information in this chapter is intended to encourage you to question, rather than just accept as Gospel the statements the Witness at your door reads to you from their own Bible.

11

NO PART OF THE WORLD

Jehovah's Witnesses, as we have seen, insist that they are not a part of Christendom. Their desire to separate themselves from others goes beyond this. The Bible records that Jesus told his apostles they were to enjoy heavenly life with him. They had been chosen out of the world, and were therefore no part of the world and because of this the world would hate them.

The apostles were no part of the world because they believed that they were destined to live in heaven. As most Witnesses expect to live forever on earth, they are part of the world in a way that only those with a heavenly hope can claim not to be. They look forward to a time when the world of mankind is destroyed and they as sole survivors become the world of mankind.

It must be remembered that at the time of Christ, Christianity had not established itself in the world. Palestine was under pagan Roman occupation and Israel was of the Jewish faith. The Witnesses try to act as though they are in the same situation and still see themselves as surrounded by hostile nations ready to persecute them. They see the governments as satanic rulers shortly to be destroyed by God. They are often reminded by their leaders that they may be tortured for their faith shortly before Armageddon. There are many other ways in which they try to create a gulf between themselves and those around them.

Voting
Jehovah's Witnesses will not involve themselves in politics at

any level. They will not salute the flag, stand for the National Anthem or run for office. Even voting at local elections is forbidden.

These actions are seen as idolatry. They say they have given their vote to Jehovah's kingdom. To support any man-made government is seen as a conflict of interest. They quote the words of Jesus, "My kingdom is no part of this world." Despite this, they do support government by paying their taxes.

The Watchtower Society and its followers are awaiting the return of Jesus, and look forward to his government ruling the earth under the supervision of Jehovah God. Meanwhile we have to have some sort of administration in each country. Some countries are fortunate enough to be democratically run and choose who will represent them.

When we vote for a party we are not voting for them to rule the world, we are merely choosing them to decide on local matters for a while. If they fail to spend our taxes wisely, then we have the opportunity of voting differently next time. Any power these officials have is given to them by the taxes we pay, whether or not we vote. Do we not have a responsibility to exercise some control over how that power is used, by voting?

Witnesses will respond to this by explaining that to vote for a government, is to support any involvement they have in war. What of the government they look forward to ruling the earth? According to their literature it will seize power by force, killing most of the human race and then be overseen by "Jehovah of Armies." From then on, the penalty for any resistance from civilians is to be instant death. What they have voted for is a military dictatorship under which all human rights will be abolished.

The reality is that whichever government is in power, it will use force in the defence of its nation. The Witnesses have already registered their stand on the issue of warfare and avoid any participation. Some of their taxes will be spent on defence whether they vote or not but there are many other social responsibilities that government carries out.

It is only due to the efforts of millions of non-Witnesses, who do involve themselves, that the Witnesses are able to enjoy the benefits of living in a well-ordered society. They are only able to stand back and enjoy the illusion of being no part of the world because others assume the responsibility for them. The reality of running a country has to be dealt with in the present.

Whenever an issue arises that involves only the Witnesses and there is no one else to lobby for change on their behalf, they will immediately involve themselves, breaking the law if necessary.

Often Witnesses will cite the example of the three Hebrews who refused to bow down to Nebuchadnezzar. They cite this as a Biblical example of how to view rulers. The circumstances of this account are quite different. The King brought the Hebrews to the inauguration of a gold image. They were commanded to fall down and worship the pagan image on pain of death. (Daniel 3:5) This historic account really has nothing to do with the selection of a civil government, which allows freedom of worship.

Jehovah's Witnesses have no interest in present governments because they already have a government of their own. The Watchtower Society issues laws, makes judgements, appoints leaders and controls every aspect of their lives, even over-ruling the law of the land if they see fit. They have voted for the Watchtower Society, which does not welcome the efforts of politicians to influence their members.

The Society seeks total control, and looks forward to the day when all governments are destroyed, leaving them to assist with the world's administration. The masthead of the Watchtower magazine states that it is non-political. This statement has to be examined closely in view of the fact that members of the Governing Body, along with many thousands of other members, expect to rule from heaven as kings. Some of the elders expect to be princes on earth. This means that they consider themselves to be part of a Royal Family. If, say, the British Royal Family started to publish statements saying that all governments were evil and due to be destroyed by God, to make way for rule by them, would the present British political parties consider their statements to be non-political?

Their claim to political neutrality is based on the idea that they are against all governments except their own. This idea is not new. Throughout history world leaders have desired to be part of an all-conquering world Empire, Dynasty or Reich but they never claimed to be non-political.

For a Witness to support any political party, other than the Watchtower Society, would be considered an act of treason. The Witnesses' stance on this, and many other anti-establishment issues, is only feasible for a small group. Their opting out of the system would not be possible were it not for the order that is afforded by the organized efforts of society as a whole.

Stop Press – The following change of policy has now been introduced

Under the heading "Questions from Readers" in a recent *Watchtower*, the Society stated :

> As to whether they will personally vote for someone running in an election, each one of Jehovah's Witnesses makes a decision based on his Bible-trained conscience and an understanding of his responsibility to God and the state…There may be people who are stumbled when they observe that during an election in their country, some Witnesses of Jehovah go to the polling booth and others do not. They may say that 'Jehovah Witnesses are not consistent.' People should recognize, though, that in matters of individual conscience such as this, each Christian has to make his own decision before Jehovah God
>
> THE WATCHTOWER – 1 NOVEMBER 1999 – PAGES 27,28

This sudden change of policy came as a surprise to the membership. Over the years the Society have quoted scripture to support their ban on voting. Does this mean that Jehovah's Witnesses will now as a group vote at elections? How can they now disregard the "scriptural proof" that was used for many decades to support their ruling? If this issue is a matter of conscience, why was it made into law and enforced for so long? Could this be another attempt by the Society to conform to The Human Rights Act, as it is fundamentally against the law to deny people the right to vote in a democracy?

What of the many who left or refused to become Witnesses because of the original ruling? By saying that voting is now a matter of conscience there is no conflict with the law of the land. In some countries it is against the law to abstain from voting and this has caused many difficulties for members. In some countries, such as Malawi members lost their lives at the hands of the authorities because they refused to vote.

Is this really a genuine change of direction or will it continue to be made clear that a properly trained Christian conscience will stop one from voting? The Watchtower article just quoted from, made it clear that members should stay separate from the world and listed five "factors" to be considered when making what is now a personal decision.

It appears that although voting is now officially allowed, the practice of voting will continue to be frowned upon, and Jehovah's Witnesses as a group will continue to avoid voting, as a matter of conscience. There are a lot of question marks above, which sums up the present position that Witnesses find themselves in. The Society claim that truth is a bright light that is getting brighter and brighter but as in this case, and the position with regard to the use of blood fractions (dealt with in chapter 13) the light or guidance seems to be getting dimmer.

All the Benefits

The Watchtower Society and its members enjoy all the benefits that being a part of an organized consumer society brings. The members are employed by the system and in some cases live on social security payments. The Society utilises the most efficient literature production and transportation systems the capitalist world has developed.

Jehovah's Witnesses benefit daily from the efficient running of schools, food production and emergency services. They are at the forefront in using law courts and governmental law to support their freedom and uphold their human rights. Not only do they benefit from medical advances, but expect preferential treatment to enable operations and organ transplants without blood transfusion. Despite benefiting from the efforts of professional people, they strongly discourage their own members from pursuing higher education.

Giving to charity is discouraged. All donations are expected to go to the Society, as this is considered the most worthy cause. They quote Jesus' words "You will always have the poor," as good reason for not giving to the under-privileged. All such assistance is reserved for those in their "nation."

115

They are no part of the world, in as much as they will not vote or help to organize local government. They are encouraged to avoid training for professional positions and, if possible, full-time work. In terms of receiving the benefits that come from the efforts of others who are not standing back waiting for the world system to end, so that they can inherit the world, they are very much a part of the world.

Mind Control

When one is a member of a group such as Jehovah's Witnesses, it is not possible to be aware of the degree to which personal freedoms that are normally taken for granted are lost. The mind-control techniques used by the Watchtower Society are by no means unique. Part of the process includes creating an atmosphere of isolation from society and a policy of non-involvement in the running of many of the institutions that are a part of normal society. Many books have been written about cults and the way that those belonging to them are controlled and manipulated. Of course those under such control are always offended at the notion that they are involved with a cult.

Steve Hassan, an ex-Moonie has written a number of books exposing the cult mind control methods. He has devised a set of guidelines that any religion can be measured against to decide whether or not a particular sect can be deemed a cult.

He divides the process of mind control into four basic categories :

(1) **Behaviour Control**
(2) **Information Control**
(3) **Thought Control**
(4) **Emotional Control**

Some of the methods used are briefly summarised below :

(1) **Behaviour Control** includes, among many things, dictating to the members how they dress and groom themselves. How much time is spent on recreation and how much time is committed to receiving indoctrination. They are expected to ask

permission before making major decisions. Information is distorted to make it acceptable to them and rigid rules are laid down. Individualism is discouraged and obedience is demanded.

(2)   Information Control includes discouraging the reading of non-cult literature and information that is critical towards the group. Keeping members too busy to have time to think clearly about what they are doing and insisting they have nothing to do with ex-members. Past sins are used to pressure and control members. The leaders decide how much information the group needs and expect members to report other's misdemeanours.

(3)   Thought Control includes the group accepting the stated beliefs as "truth." They are trained to see themselves in a good-versus-evil situation where every issue is simply black or white. Key words are adopted and used as "buzz words." No criticism of the leaders or their doctrine is permitted and all alternative religious groups are seen as bad.

(4)   Emotional Control includes using any guilt they may feel about their thoughts, feelings, family or their past. Any problems individuals may be experiencing are to be seen as the fault of the one who has the problems. Fear is built up in the minds of the members by warning them of the dangers of the "outside" world and the enemies that surround them. Fear of losing the approval of the other members is a key factor in pressuring the members to continue. The members are indoctrinated to fear questioning the leaders or being made to leave the group as they are told they will have no future if they are outside the safety of the group. There is no legitimate reason for leaving and those that do must be shunned. Without the protection of the group they could be exposed to possession by demons.

As you can see from the length of the last paragraph, fear is a prominent factor in keeping members of cults in line. As stated, these guidelines were not written with Jehovah's Witnesses specifically in mind. These guidelines can be applied to any sect to determine whether or not that sect or religion is a cult.

The Watchtower Society's Armageddon

The Watchtower Society teaches that Armageddon is a literal

battle and an execution. Anyone not protected by association with them is to be executed. This is to include the children of non-Witnesses. Many Witnesses will also be killed, because they are constantly being reminded that only those who are "whole-souled" will be spared. Fear of such a death is the reason for many members staying in line. The threat of death at Armageddon is a constant feature of Watchtower literature and a major control method due to the high level of fear it creates among the membership :

> May we never be tempted to venture into the danger zone for whatever reason our mind might come up with, since the day we cross the line back into the world could be the day of Jehovah.
>
> *THE WATCHTOWER* – 15 FEBRUARY 2000 – PAGE 7

The Witnesses number less than 0.1% of the world's population. If they were all to be spared, more than 99.9% of the people on earth would still perish. Their literature tells us, many times, that they will watch the execution and applaud.

With so many billions of dead corpses around, it is likely that the ensuing disease would kill off the survivors. Who would care for the millions of domestic pets and milk the dairy cows? Who would find time to comfort any survivors, including children, who have enough heart to be in a state of shock at the loss of almost the whole of humanity? How can a group of people, who consider themselves more worthy of life than others, be disappointed that such a horrendous calamity has not yet been inflicted on the human race?

If this slaughter were to take place, most Witnesses would have just lost most, if not all, of their relatives. When one becomes aware of the revulsion that most people feel towards genocide, such as was authorised by Hitler, it is hard to see how a group of people can look forward with eager anticipation to such a slaughter. Who would want to live in a world that is ruled by someone capable of commanding such a slaughter? How could any survivor then enjoy life, in a world that has paid such a high price for daring to believe that the Watchtower Society was not a reliable organization in which to put faith?

The remaining Witnesses would then have to spend the rest

of eternity knowing that any mistake on their part would result in their execution at the hand of the God whom they still love. They believe that providing they can make it through the first thousand years they will reach perfection, after which they are not likely to sin. The problem is that they also believe that the first man and woman, Adam and Eve, were perfect but turned against God. The perfect angel who was sent to look after them also sinned and became Satan the Devil. What makes them think it will be any easier to keep all the rules in a new world than it was in paradise? It doesn't look good!

To make things even more difficult the Witnesses believe that the Devil will be released at the end of the thousand years :

He will again try to mislead humans, some of whom will choose independence from God. To prevent 'distress from rising a second time,' Jehovah will annihilate Satan, his demons and all who rebel against Jehovah's sovereignty. No one could object that any humans who are destroyed eternally at that time did not have a chance or that their wrong course was due to imperfection. No, they will be like Adam and Eve, who willingly chose to rebel against Jehovah's righteous rule.

THE WATCHTOWER – 15 OCTOBER 2000 – PAGE 19

The members of the Governing Body decided, many years ago, that they were to go to heaven the instant they died, to be rewarded with, not just everlasting life immediately, but also immortality. No more testing, no chance of death or failing but guaranteed positions as kings and priests in heaven. To a casual observer, it could appear that the membership on the whole have drawn a short straw.

Although any member can decide that they are of the heavenly calling, surprisingly, the number of those who think they are of "the anointed" has remained constant for around ten years. The reluctance of ordinary members to come forward could be due to the belief that any who partake unworthily of the emblems at the Lord's Supper will pay with their lives. As no one can really be sure how they are supposed to feel if they have been chosen, the majority accept that they are destined to live on earth.

Who would Jesus and the 144,000 chosen members chosen to go to heaven as kings rule over? They claim that the destruction will make way for a resurrection, which will take place during 1,000 years of peace. The Witnesses are aware that the Bible says :

> These came to life again and reigned with Christ for a thousand years, though the rest of the dead did not come to life until the thousand years were over. This is the first resurrection. Happy indeed, and one of God's own people, is the man who shares in this first resurrection! Upon such the second death has no claim; but they shall be priests of God and Christ, and shall reign for the thousand years.   REVELATION 20:4-6

This is confusing because the Witnesses believe that their chosen members were resurrected to heaven in 1919, and yet this was not followed by 1,000 years of peace. In any case the matter in hand is – who will these kings rule over? The few Witnesses who have been spared could hardly be called "the nations" that the Bible says Jesus and his kings are to shepherd. The Society is aware of this discrepancy and explain that the scripture does not mean what it says.

Coming to life to rule as kings is literal. The rest of the dead coming to life at the end of the thousand years is symbolic. The rest of the dead are in fact resurrected during the thousand years but given imperfect bodies. This means God would have to deliberately create defective people. Those that apply themselves will slowly grow towards perfection. The others will grow old again and die. Those that make it to the end of the thousand years will reach perfection. Life is supposed to refer to perfect life on earth. It is there to be had, and those that reach the end of the millennium will reach it. In this sense they "come to life."

Do you see how simple the Bible can be when the Watchtower Society explains it?

The Bible does not teach that God plans to slaughter billions of people in Christian and non-Christian countries. Christians believe that Jesus will rule the world, not destroy it. To execute the whole world of mankind, except the Witnesses, would show they had already been judged. According to the Bible, judgement takes place after death!

There is no reason for whole civilisations to be destroyed because they failed to attend Watchtower Society meetings, or read all their latest publications. Millions of people around the world have never even been offered a Watchtower. If the nations of the world are not to be wiped out, then what does the Bible claim Jesus will do?

And he will certainly render judgment among the nations and set matters straight respecting many peoples. And they will have to beat their swords into plowshares. Nation will not lift up sword against nation; neither will they learn war any more.

ISAIAH 2:4 – NWT

And to him the kings will prostrate themselves; all the nations, for their part, will serve him. PSALMS 72:11 – NWT

Fear is only as real as we allow it to be in our minds.
By learning not to fear death, we cease fearing life,
And once fear is gone, there is room for love.
Once we have come to know love, we are whole,
Then truth will seek us out.

* * *

12

PAGAN CELEBRATIONS

Among the many ways in which Jehovah's Witnesses set themselves apart from Christendom, is their refusal to celebrate Birthdays, Easter or Christmas. They also refuse to recognise any of the days appointed to the various saints, as these are said to be part of pagan worship. Surprisingly their Society does allow the celebration of anniversaries. The celebration of Easter is forbidden. They state: "Did Christ give a command to celebrate his resurrection? No, he did not."

THE TRUTH THAT LEADS TO ETERNAL LIFE – Page 147

Birthdays

The Bible only records two birthday celebrations. Pharaoh of Egypt had all the first-born babies killed on his birthday, and Herod Antipas had John the Baptist beheaded on his. The Society argue that out of respect for those that lost their lives on birthdays, their members should avoid happy celebration of their own birthdays and those of their children. Anyone who disobeys is disfellowshipped.

The other reason given is that birthday celebrations "exalt" the one whose birthday it is and makes him or her the centre of attention rather than God.

THE TRUTH THAT LEADS TO ETERNAL LIFE – Page 146

These seem rather vague reasons for expelling members from

the "spiritual paradise" costing them their chance of everlasting life. As there is no scriptural prohibition against celebrating birthdays, what is the charge on which offenders are disfellowshipped? Well, on the occasions that I witnessed members being expelled in this way, the charge of apostasy was used!

You may wonder how throwing a birthday party for one's child or attending a party to celebrate the birth of Christ can be deemed apostasy? Well, as the Watchtower Society has decided that its members must not recognise birthdays, to do so is an act of disobedience towards them and a challenge to their authority. The charge then is one of apostasy against the Society. As they believe that they speak for God himself, the offence is viewed as disobedience towards God.

I am sorry if you find it difficult to follow this reasoning but so did the friends of mine that were disfellowshipped on this charge. Their crime was to hold a small private birthday party for their little girl. The little girl in her excitement told the child of another Witness. This child's parents duly reported the infringement of the rules to the elders. Both parents said they felt they had done nothing unscriptural but were disfellowshipped the same week and then shunned by the congregation. They were so appalled by their treatment that they remained outside the organization and decided to prayerfully seek "the truth" elsewhere.

If the elders were not to stamp out such conduct, just think of the consequences. The idea could catch on and children throughout the Witness movement could suddenly find themselves celebrating their birthdays and being made to feel special for one day each year!

As with so many other Society rules it may be only a matter of time before the rules are changed. This will be of little comfort to those parents who were thrown out for breaching Society law or the children who have grown up without ever having a birthday party or attending one held by their friends.

Christmas

Members who celebrate Christmas are also disfellowshipped. Christmas is celebrated on the same day of the year as the

Romans used to celebrate Saturnalia - the birth of the sun. It is also a birthday. For these reasons, the Witnesses consider it to be a totally pagan festival. They also state that God has not commanded Christians to celebrate the birth of Christ, it is his death that is important. Do these factors make it wrong for Christians to celebrate the birth of their king?

Supposing a Christian left the faith and chose the same date for the celebration of a pagan festival that he had previously used for a Christian festival. Would we not say that he had gone too far, that he was adding insult to injury? His pagan god would see it as a triumph, not a compromise.

The idea of a birthday, according to the Society, is to exalt the person concerned and make them the centre of attention. Is there a better way for Christians to exalt their Lord than to celebrate his birthday on a day previously used to exalt a pagan god?

If Christians had been commanded to celebrate the birth of Jesus there would be little merit in doing so. A spontaneous gesture is far more significant.

Not Commanded to Celebrate Christ's Birth

Should Christians be forbidden from celebrating the birth of Jesus or any other event because they cannot find a specific command in the Bible to do so? Is the Society being consistent?

For decades the Society has arranged vast assemblies around the world for its members. They have tried to draw a parallel between these gatherings and the "festival of booths" that the Israelites celebrated annually. It is unthinkable for members to miss these annual events, and yet, early Christians did not hold such gatherings.

Most of the Witnesses activities are not even mentioned in the Bible. They have been stipulated by their Society because it considers them to be appropriate. The Watchtower Society has devoted numerous books to the remembrance of its important dates, such as 1914, 1918 and 1919 and repeated its version of the events of these years, countless times. The birthdays, life stories and dates of death of their founders are highlighted continually.

The Christian church wishes to proclaim the birth of its king, and relive the events surrounding the birth of one whom they consider to be the most important baby ever born. There is no scriptural command to do this nor is there a prohibition against it. It is what Christians consider appropriate.

There is no room in the Society for individuals to decide for themselves the merits of Christmas. Any member who wishes to remember the birth of their king in this way is dismissed from the spiritual nation to await their death at Armageddon.

Could it be that the idea of millions of sincere men and women attending church to honour Christ without joining their nation is hard to accept. This is not what the Society desire. They wish the attention to go to Jehovah, as they claim to direct his nation. By convincing its members that Christmas and Easter are part of pagan worship they are able to condemn the Christian church. It is further proof to their members that they are a sacred nation surrounded by heathens.

Pagan Customs that are accepted

The Watchtower Society's reason for condemning so many activities is that they have pagan origins. As pagans populated the earth for at least 4,000 years, by the Society's reckoning, before Christ came, there is almost nothing that can be done that has not already been done by pagans. Incidentally, they only became pagans when the Roman Empire adopted Christianity. Until then they were just people!

Among other pagan customs accepted by the Society are wedding receptions, wedding cakes, the lighting of candles, white wedding dresses, bridesmaids, wedding rings, ear-rings, honeymoons and so on. Strangely, the throwing of confetti is singled out as pagan and strictly forbidden. The wearing of a beard is heavily frowned upon. Are they aware that shaving is a totally pagan Egyptian and Greek custom, adopted by the Romans, but unheard of among Israelites and the early Christians?

The early Christians disagreed over which festivals and customs they should observe, so Apostle Paul said: "Therefore let no man judge you in eating and drinking or in respect of a festival or of an observance of the new moon or of a Sabbath." (Colossians 2:16 – NWT)

Whatever the origin of our various customs, it is how they are viewed today, and the motive behind observing them in the present that is relevant. Folk law, custom and heritage, impinge on every aspect of life, even the language we speak. So how do the Watchtower Society decide on these matters with such inconsistency, and why are such opinions made into law?

Enter the Spider

The belief system of the Witnesses is based on the premise that the world is not as it should be. They believe that the world has fallen out of favour with God and exists in a state of imperfection. Not only is mankind out of favour, but also the whole of the natural world of animals, birds, fish, insects and so on. They believe that animals have always died of old age. It is only humans who die of old age as a result of falling out with God.

In the original paradise, before Adam and Eve sinned, all creatures ate vegetation as none of them were designed to hunt or eat meat. This would mean that mean that prior to humans, the earth would have been inhabited by millions of creatures with no predators to control their numbers. As they died there would be no meat eating birds and insects to dispose of their carcasses. What happened to them? The potential for disease must have been enormous.

Let's examine the humble spider and follow this through. The spider is an amazing creature, designed to produce and spin thread to make a web so wonderfully constructed that scientists have referred to it as a miracle. The spider's eight legs enable it to walk on the web and still have spare legs to tie up its prey, which the web is designed to catch.

The Witnesses do not believe that evolution plays any part in the process by which animals come to be as they are. This means that God must have carefully designed the spider in its present form. This presents a difficulty, as the Witnesses believe that God rested from his creative work after he had made Adam and Eve. This "day of rest" is said to be 7,000 years long and include the time we are presently living in.

Did God then start creating again on his "day of rest?" Why would a loving God deliberately sabotage his own paradise and recreate the spider to trap and kill other insects, just because Adam and Eve displeased him?

For the Witnesses' beliefs to hold true the whole of creation would have had to be recreated. Lions and tigers recreated with claws and flesh-eating teeth, zebras recreated with stripes to camouflage them against predators, eagles given talons to carry off prey and flesh-tearing beaks to eat with. Sharks recreated with perfect rows of teeth to eat other fish. Then there are the plants that eat insects to consider. Were they also recreated to do this?

A good look at a few nature programmes is enough to make it clear that the whole of nature and the food chain is a carefully balanced work of art, in which every living and dead creature has a part to play.

As Witnesses believe the animal kingdom had been in existence for many thousands of years before the creation of Adam and Eve, eating vegetation, with no natural enemies to reduce their numbers, there must have been hundreds of millions of animals, fish, birds and insects. Recreating them would have been a huge task, bigger than the Bible's account of the original creation. Did God really do all this on his "day of rest," and why?

The sum is so vast that it will simplify things if we just apply the question to the spider. If the spider was not originally created to eat other insects, and evolution is to be ruled out, how did it come to be? The Witnesses claim it just happened as a result of Adam and Eve sinning. The difficulty is that they also claim that nothing in creation just happens or evolves, but everything is the result of careful design by God. They see creation as an event fixed in time, rather than an intelligent process.

Does it matter when the spider came to exist in its present form? Well the original claim being examined is that the world, including the animal kingdom, is not as it was meant to be. If the spider and all other creatures were not recreated after humans, on God's "day of rest," then we are left with only one alternative. The spider was always a spider in its many hundreds of forms. Its web is indeed a miracle and it is as it was meant to be.

There is huge significance to this. As you have already concluded, what applies to the spider also applies to the whole of the animal kingdom and the natural world. It is as good as it can be, and does not represent a failure on the part of a creator. Rather the natural world is a marvellous manifestation of life on a physical plane. Life in the physical world does involve pain and death. That is the nature of the corporeal world. The animal kingdom does not represent a world gone wrong or deliberately recreated in an imperfect way by a cruel God, who had originally managed to make a world free from suffering.

If a Jehovah's Witness is able to take an honest look at the natural world and conclude that it cannot possibly have come into being twice, once perfectly, and then imperfectly, he or she would then have to conclude that the idea that God will recreate the world for a third time, to turn it back to the way it was the first time, as Paradise restored, is not really feasible. We could ask why he is going to change the very nature of wild beasts so they can live as peaceful herbivores in "paradise restored" and yet kill off most of the human race?

Perfect harmony already exists in the natural world. Nature accepts the pain along with the joy because the joy of existence outweighs the pain. It is not possible to have only joy in a physical world. Joy and pain are two sides of the same coin. The natural world is already a wonderful and worthy expression of life on earth. It continues to do what it has always done, that is to improve and advance. It adapts and advances basing its progress on the experience it has accumulated. Not only humans do this but all living things. Why? Because they are alive and they hold within themselves the intelligence that is contained in the life force.

If a Witness is able to accept that the animal kingdom is not an imperfect failure but a success, then he or she may be able to look with less disapproval at the human race. Despite all our failings, we are as a race making progress. Life on earth is as good as it can be. There is huge room for us as humans to improve, but if we look around realistically, life is improving for most humans. We have a long way to go, and our journey will involve suffering, but humans are brave and wonderful creatures who will meet the challenges of the future. In the human spirit, God has expressed himself. God has not failed and nor will the human race.

Truth never changes, only opinions change.
Letting go of the old makes way for the new.
Isn't this the lesson that nature teaches us?
The world was never flat – it is us that changed.
Willingness to change allows room for growth.

✳ ✳ ✳

13

RESPECT FOR BLOOD

Jehovah's Witnesses are well known for their refusal to accept blood transfusions. They are required to carry a "No Blood Tansfusion Card." Even when faced with death, they will not recant as this issue is seen as a test of faith. To break this law results in disfellowshipping. The idea that blood is sacred is found in the Bible.

> For the soul of every sort of flesh is in its blood by the soul in it. Consequently I said to the sons of Israel: "You must not eat the blood of any sort of flesh, because the soul of every sort of flesh is its blood. Anyone eating it will be cut off."
>
> LEVITICUS 17:14 – NWT

This command to the Israelites shows the principle behind not using blood as food. When an animal's life had been taken, the blood was to be left as a reminder that all life belongs to God – the giver of life. The Society accept that this applied to the Israelites, who believed themselves to have a law covenant with God but refer to the words of Apostle Paul, addressed to Christians :

> For the holy spirit and we ourselves have favoured adding no further burden to you, except these necessary things, to keep abstaining from things sacrificed to idols and from blood and from things strangled and from fornication. If you keep your-selves from these things, you will prosper. Good health to you!
>
> ACTS 15:28,29 – NWT

Why did Apostle Paul feel the need to mention blood? At the time, the Jews were under Roman occupation. The Roman practice was to drink animal blood. To the Jews, this showed disrespect for the principle that the life belonged to God. Drinking blood was a practice that Jews and Christians avoided.

Human Blood

The Bible has much to say about human blood. Christians believe that Jesus poured out his blood on behalf of mankind. His disciples drank red wine, which symbolised his blood. Jesus' disciples who were both Jews and Christians knew they had been instructed not to drink blood, so why would they simulate this? Because Jesus had instructed them to do this, to show that they wanted to benefit from the sacrifice of his life.

> Accordingly Jesus said to them: " Most truly I say to you, unless you eat the flesh of the son of man and drink his blood, you have no life in yourselves. He that feeds on my flesh and drinks my blood has everlasting life, and I shall resurrect him at the last day; for my flesh is truly food, and my blood is true drink."
>
> JOHN 6:53-55 – NWT

How did those early Christians reconcile the symbolically drinking blood with the clear scriptural prohibition not to drink blood? They were symbolically drinking Christ's human blood, which they believed would save their lives. They were showing respect for the principle that the life is in the blood. Blood cannot have greater value than life itself. To a Christian, the only proper use for blood is to save life.

The early Christians were aware that it was unscriptural to drink blood, they also realized that the principle involved was respect for God and life. There was no conflict in their minds, as the symbolic drinking of Jesus' blood was not showing disrespect for the sacredness of blood, quite the opposite.

Blood Transfusion

So is it unscriptural for Jehovah's Witnesses to receive blood transfusions? Christians believe that Jesus gave his life for others, but do they have the right to do the same?

No one has greater love that this, that someone should surrender his soul in behalf of his friends.   JOHN 15:13 – NWT

According to the Bible Christians do have the right to give their
lives so that others may live. If Christians can give their lives,
would it be consistent to view some of their spare blood as
more sacred than another's life? The Society believes that the
Bible's comments on blood make not just blood transfusions a
sin but also the use of any blood parts.

For some time it was unclear whether a Witness was allowed
to have his or her own blood stored before an operation and
then transfused as needed. This matter was clarified ten months
into this new century :

> In the light of Bible commands about the proper use of blood,
> how do Jehovah's Witnesses view medical procedures using
> one's own blood?
>
> Blood is not to be stored: it is to be poured out – returned to
> God, as it were. Granted, the Mosaic law is not in force now.
> Nevertheless, Jehovah's Witnesses respect the principles God
> included in it, and they are determined to 'abstain from blood.'
> Hence we do not donate blood, nor do we store for transfusion
> our blood that should be 'poured out.' That practice conflicts
> with God's law. *THE WATCHTOWER* – 15 OCTOBER 2000 – PAGES 30,31

The article goes on to explain that in procedures such as hemod-
ilution in which the blood leaves the patient's body and flows
back would be up to the individual's conscience. The same
would apply to allowing the blood to flow through a machine
before returning. More difficult is the idea of having blood
taken for a sample and then stored. How is this any different
from storing one's own blood for an operation, the practice of
which has been outlawed by the Society?

Most Witnesses will accept the use of cardio-pulmonary
bypass, dialysis, intra-operative blood salvage, and re-infusion.
As modern science advances and more treatments become
available, many members will no doubt find it difficult to work
it all out and are likely to find themselves trying to do so when
they are ill.

To add to the confusion is the situation that has developed in Bulgaria. With the increase in attention to human rights there is growing concern regarding the Watchtower Society's ban on blood transfusions. Few Witnesses are aware of the 1998 case between the Watchtower Society and the Bulgarian government. To settle the case, they signed a legally binding document giving Witnesses freedom of choice regarding blood transfusions. In the statement that follows the applicant is the Watchtower Society :

> The applicant undertook with regard to its stance on blood transfusions to draft a statement for inclusion in its statute providing that members should have free choice in the matter for themselves and their children, without any control or sanction on the part of the association.   APPLICANT NO 28626/95

Are the Witnesses abiding by this Bulgarian undertaking or covertly undermining the promised freedom of choice? Will this ruling become worldwide or will the Witnesses in Bulgaria be treated differently to the others?

The Bible sets out many principles to guide those who wish to live as Christians. Does the Watchtower Society have the right to make its opinion into law?

They have not always ruled that blood transfusions are wrong. At one time, the Society ruled that vaccinations and organ transplants were wrong but later changed their mind. Recently the Society informed all elders that those members who accepted a blood transfusion were not to be automatically disfellowshipped. This change of policy was not made known to the ordinary members. This change may well have been the result of pressure to conform to the legal requirements of The Human Rights Act.

Until recently the Society had insisted that the use of all blood parts such as red or white cells including hemoglobin, plasma and platelets were also banned. To accept any such treatments was the same as having a transfusion. This ruling was based on the Biblical admonition to "abstain from blood." Now they have decided that some of these blood parts can be used!

Members in the USA are expected to fill in a "Durable Power

of Attorney" and distribute this legal document to friends, relatives and their doctor so that in the case of an accident, the hospital would know that they were not to give the injured person a blood transfusion.

On 1 December 2000, elders in the USA were informed in writing by the Society that in line with articles appearing in both 15 June 2000 and 15 October 2000 Watchtower magazines, the DPA forms had been amended to allow members to accept the previously forbidden fractionated blood parts.

Using the name Lee Elder, the founder of AJWRB, a group that has been set up to determine the feelings of Witnesses regarding the ban on blood, stated the following :

> Even more significant is this further comment from the Watchtower Society: "only a small percentage of the brothers have filled out the Society's DPA form." This recent statement from the Watchtower Society is very important in that it shows that level of commitment to the Watchtower Society policy is very small. If a Jehovah's Witness is unconscious and exsanguinating and no DPA can be presented, I believe a very strong argument exists that the person is not committed to the Watchtower Society policy. Especially in light of this recent disclosure by the Watchtower Society, which reveals dwindling support for its partial blood policy. It is also noteworthy that nearly a year after ceasing its policy of disfellowshiping Jehovah's Witnesses who accept blood or the blood products that are still forbidden; the Watchtower Society has never informed the general membership of the change. Only the congregation elders have been informed to date. WWW.AJWRB.ORG

One elder, writing under the pseudonym Mr Shilmer, to avoid disciplinary action has asked the Watchtower's head office to justify this turn-around and clarify the position. A copy of his letter was sent to The Regional Ethics Council in Portland USA. A reply was received from Dr Osamu Muramoto, which reads in part :

> I appreciate Mr. Shilmer's comment as an active Witness elder. Compared with Mr. Bartlett's letter, the opinions of Mr.Shilmer and Mr. Elder testify how diverse the views are on this issue

among Jehovah's Witnesses. Since Mr. Shilmer raised the question of partial abstinence from blood, I would like to add one example to show how the new WTS blood policy is NOT abstaining from blood.

As I stated in this paper, and as clearly stated in the new version of the Durable Power of Attorney form printed by the WTS and distributed to the JWs in the United States last week, the new policy allows JWs to accept "all fractions" of "any primary component." The WTS has emphasized in its literature that those "fractions" are "small" and therefore acceptable.

When I ask JWs why those "fractions" are acceptable, most would reply, "because they are tiny fractions." Under this new policy, the most important "fraction" JWs are now permitted to accept is hemoglobin-based blood substitutes, which had been prohibited until recently. How "small" is hemoglobin as a fraction of the blood? Let me quote a simple sentence from a college-level anatomy textbook: "Discounting its water content, an erythrocyte [red blood cells, which WTS determined unacceptable] is over 97% hemoglobin, the molecule that binds to and transports respiratory gasses."

REFERENCE 1. MARIEB E. *HUMAN ANATOMY AND PHYSIOLOGY*. 4TH ED.
MENLO PARK, CA:ADDISON WESLEY LONGMAN INC; 1998:630

If God commands to abstain from red blood cells, as the WTS teaches, why does the WTS also teach that accepting 97% of what God prohibits does not violate God's command?

US SPELLING

As the Society have changed their mind on so many other verses of scripture, and applied the scriptures on this matter in so many different ways, perhaps they will change their mind on this issue completely. If they do, it will be of no comfort to the relatives of those who have died as a result of their ruling.

More critically for the Society, these changes further undermine their claim that they have been appointed by holy spirit to dispense accurate knowledge which they insist the members eternal lives depend upon. By making the Bible's comments on the use of animal blood into a law regarding the life-saving use of human blood, have they carried out their "duty of care" towards the present lives of their members?

The Lord's Supper

Originally the Israelites celebrated the annual Passover festival, which was a feast of which everyone partook. The Bible accounts record that Jesus used this occasion, just prior to his death, to declare a New Covenant with his disciples in which they would join him in heaven. This pact was to be based on the sacrificial shedding of his blood.

Jesus Christ showed his followers how to symbolise their involvement by symbolically eating his flesh and drinking his blood. The emblems of bread and wine stand for the body and blood of Christ. They symbolise the Christian New Covenant. Christians see no conflict between the Bible's prohibition on the drinking of animal blood and Christ's command to eat his flesh and drink his blood.

The Lord's Supper or Holy Communion is the way by which Christians signify that they want to receive Christ's body and share in the promises made. What was originally called the Passover became the Lord's Supper after the intervention of Jesus. Jehovah's Witnesses refer to this ceremony as "The Memorial."

The following is a reference to the manna or bread, which the Israelites are said to have miraculously received while in the wilderness. Jesus is saying that his body, represented by the bread, must be eaten to gain everlasting life :

> I am that living bread which has come down from heaven: if anyone eats this bread he shall live for ever...This is the bread which came down from heaven; and it is not like the bread which our forefathers ate: they are dead, but whoever eats this bread shall live forever.   SEE JOHN 6:51-58 FOR FULL TEXT – NWT

The Society states that it is not necessary for their ordinary members to eat this bread, because association with them is enough. They draw a comparison between the way the Israelites were joined by the Jonadabs and Gibeonites – neighbouring nations who shared Israel's prosperity by association. Of course the Israelites vastly out numbered these nations, unlike the great crowd of Witnesses they are supposed to represent.

To Watch is enough

The Bible clearly states that all who partake of the emblems at the Lord's Supper will join Jesus in heaven. The ceremony is representative of a new covenant between Christ and Christians.

The Watchtower Society has a problem with this. Those who partake hope to go to heaven. Nearly all Witnesses expect to stay on earth. Out of all the people who have ever lived on earth, they believe only 144,000 will go to heaven. Around 8,000 of these are believed to be alive today, all of them Witnesses. These are allowed to take the emblems, just once a year.

As all other Witnesses have been told they will not go to heaven, they are forbidden to partake. For them to do so would be considered "partaking unworthily," and they are warned that this could cost them their lives. So how do they believe they benefit from this arrangement?

They are allowed to watch the chosen few in their congregation partake at an annual event called "the memorial". By watching them partake, they believe they qualify to live forever on earth. They are called observers. What if none of these chosen ones are in their congregation? In this event, the commemoration takes place in the same way, but no one, not even those taking the ceremony partake of the emblems. The wine and the bread are passed around and return to the table untouched. The members present are not even able to watch someone else partake and claim to have been observers.

How can a Christian claim to have taken part in the Lord's Supper just by looking at the emblems? To all but the Witnesses this seems strangely removed from the example that Jesus gave Christians to follow.

To be a Witness, one is denied of partaking in the Lord's Supper with other Christians – the most fundamental act of faith a Christian can perform. All who wish to be Christians should look into the matter very seriously and decide whether the Watchtower Society's view on this matter fulfils the scriptural requirement for Christians.

14

UNDERSTANDING JEHOVAH'S WITNESSES

Maybe you are among those who have read this far because you have friends or relatives who are in some way involved with Jehovah's Witnesses and you would like to understand them better or reach out to them.

By now you will have gained a better idea of how they think and feel. You will have an insight into the belief structure that they have built their lives around. As a group they are, by choice, emotionally isolated from the world outside of their organization. In order to maintain this separateness they will avoid all unnecessary association with those who do not share their views.

Few Witnesses will read literature from other churches, even literature that is in no way directed at them. They avoid religious pamphlets, books and magazines, relying on their Society to explain to them what other churches teach. This obviously removes any possibility of seeing other churches in a sympathetic light.

The reading of literature that criticises their movement is strongly discouraged. Members are told that it is an act of disloyalty to accept such reading material. Reading literature written by an ex-member is seen as an act of apostasy, as the writer is viewed as an apostate. Repeated warnings are given from the platform and through *The Watchtower* magazine.

Satan the Devil is believed to inspire all such literature. Most Witnesses do not just avoid reading unfavourable literature but would not even allow it to be brought into their homes. Moral churchgoers are seen as a worse threat than obvious sinners. The Society warn that such people give the impression of being decent, when in fact, they are a part of Satan's organization. Witnesses are told to avoid the subtle snares that Satan lays for them in the form of such people. For a Witness to believe that wholesome and worthwhile friends can be found outside of their special nation could create a severe conflict in their minds.

Doubt is the enemy. Doubt is equated with a lack of faith. Any attempt to think through an apparent contradiction or consider even firm evidence against the Society's integrity, shows a lack of faith. To lack faith in the Society is to lack faith in God. In the mind of a Witness the Society is a physical, tangible reflection of God himself. Witnesses are repeatedly told that their perception of the Society is their perception of God. Naturally members live in fear of being out of step with the Society, which equals being out of step with God.

Anyone or anything that may put doubt in the mind of a member is to be avoided. Seasoned members will not read, listen to, or even think a word against the Society. This state of mind even prevents members from reading their Society's own literature from previous years. They will deny the Society has made certain statements, if they contradict the latest teachings. If such evidence is found in a Watchtower only a few years old, a loyal member will walk away from someone attempting to present it, rather than read something in their own Society's literature that may cause them to have doubts.

Once a member is fully involved, the years of conditioning that follow, or what some have termed brainwashing, can have a permanent effect on the mind. Many years of living by rigid rules and beliefs that can only be changed if authorised by their Society, can make the mind of Witnesses brittle. The ability to think, assimilate new information and change one's mind in an independent way is severely diminished.

The Wall

This is another factor that keeps members loyal to the Society. Ancient nations throughout history and in the Bible time of Israel protected themselves by building a wall around each city. The wall kept them safe from all outside influence and established a clear boundary. The restored Israelite nation that the Witnesses claim to be has no wall. They are an unprotected nation. Every vulnerable city must have a wall. Each Witness is helped to build his own wall. As the whole concept of their nation exists in their minds, a wall is gradually built around each mind.

As you talk to a Witness you become aware that however persuasive your argument, however irrefutable the facts you present, seldom will anything you say reach his or her mind, if they listen at all. It can be like talking to a brick wall. A normal mind will listen to all the facts and then form an opinion. Witnesses will not allow the facts into their minds, either by walking away from the attempted breach of the wall or letting the wall prevent the attempted intrusion. As far as they are concerned they already have all the facts and their commission is to convince you that they have the truth.

To reach the mind of a Witness one has to overcome this wall. Trying to take the wall down seldom works because for every brick you remove, the Witness has a counter move. In most instances the Witness can rebuild the wall faster than it can be torn down. Should you start to get through, the Witness will withdraw to the safety of the other members who will help to rebuild the wall. This is called "strengthening a weak member."

The rebuilding process involves going over the comments that damage the wall and refuting them, reminding the weakened member that loyalty to the Society is essential and shows love for Jehovah God. A member who has suffered damage to their wall will be advised to work alongside mature brothers when going from door to door. These are members whose walls are in good repair. Each time the wall is damaged, repair becomes more difficult. The Society is aware that repeated association with those outside the nation can undermine the wall. This is why members are told to avoid such friendships.

Opening the Door

In order to make the reasoning mechanism of a Witness function, the facts you have must reach the mind. If the wall cannot be penetrated, how do you reach the mind of the Witness?

You must induce the Witness to open the door in his or her wall. This door is opened wide during the many Kingdom Hall meetings and when reading Watchtower literature. It is the wall's strongest point – also its weakest if you know how to open it.

The key is to use theocratic terms. These are words, which the Society uses as triggers for whole avenues of understanding. For example; Armageddon, Babylon the Great, great crowd, Bethel, channel of communication, evil slave, faithful and discreet slave, Governing Body, Jehovah's arrangement, memorial service, new world, old world, organization-mindedness, pioneer service, theocratic society.

Using these terms will not open the door. They are just a key – they unlock the door. The Witness is trained to allow in all favourable comments towards his religion. So how should you respond to a Witness?

Perhaps you would like to know the best way to confound a Witness with some points that he or she will find impossible to refute. There is no such ready-made recipe. Unless you have studied the beliefs of Jehovah's Witnesses and are totally familiar with the scriptures they quote to support their beliefs, it is unwise to take on a trained Witness.

In any event, however convincing your argument, most Witnesses will hear very little of what you say. They are trained to appear to listen for a while, then return to the point they originally wanted to make. Trying to win on points of doctrine is usually a waste of time. The Witness will ask questions in order to establish an area that you can be proved wrong on. It is best to avoid answering questions; if say, a male Witness is trying to give you a testimony of his beliefs, it is proper for him to answer your questions.

To the Witness, the Bible is his authority. It is inconceivable to Witnesses that any other holy book could contain the truth about God and his purpose for the human race. If the Witness opens his Bible to support his view or answer your question, do not allow him to dart all over the Bible, but take the verse that he has read and insist on staying with that thought and reading the whole chapter. Usually the context will clarify the meaning. It is best to follow in your own Bible. On the whole try to avoid getting bibles out. The few minutes of discussion time do not allow for this. Quoting single verses of scripture establishes nothing. Argument and conflict must be avoided. Debate must not turn into a point scoring competition. Once the Witness has decided that you are not a threat to him, he will open the door to his mind a little because he feels you and he understand each other. This is not a trick. To converse with a Witness and achieve his trust, you really do need to understand him. Behind the wall is a caring and kind human. His intentions are honest. He is a disciplined man who cares enough to call on others to share his beliefs.

The motive for any discussion should be concern for a worthwhile person who has been misled. If he opens his mind to you, do not abuse this trust or try to hurt him. Continue to reason with him in a kind and understanding way. Attacking his organization or threatening his feeling of spiritual superiority, will cause him to slam the door to his mind.

Once a Witness begins to think, many suppressed thoughts and feelings will begin to surface. Insecurity will cause him or her to stay behind their wall while working things out. You will not be allowed into the Witness' mind for any length of time. In the brief moments while the door is open, do not try to threaten the security he or she finds in their organization but rather offer additional security. To fully understand a Witness and help them, takes time and patience. All offence at their presumption that you are soon to die at the hand of God, whom they love, while they are to be rewarded with eternal life, must be put aside. Most Witnesses are motivated far more by a fear of God than a love for him.

Jehovah's Witnesses as individuals have learned to develop a shield against each other out of fear that should they not measure up to the Society's standards, they will be reported. The Society expects them to show no favouritism to other members. There must be a uniform amount of affection to each congregation member. The Watchtower Society is an impersonal corporation. Their books and articles never bear the writer's name. The instruction and information is said to come from Jehovah God through this remote publishing company.

The number of members leaving is seen as proof that we are living in the last days as the Bible states that "the love of the greater number will cool off." When enough replacements join the organization to swell the number again, the Scripture that says, "Jehovah will speed it up in his own time" is quoted to again prove that these are the last days. Witnesses are expert at finding a verse of Scripture to support any belief they hold. In their eyes, to disagree with them is to contradict the Bible and therefore God.

Before any progress can be made towards establishing a relationship with a Witness the fear of you as a "worldling" or outsider, must be overcome by the Witness. This can only be done if you have a genuine concern towards the Witness and feel affection towards him or her as a person. Should the person you wish to help be a relative then this should come naturally.

It is difficult for someone who has never been a Jehovah's Witness to fully comprehend how totally committed most members are. Keeping up with the demands of a modern world and the demands of their religion can cause severe stress. To remain a Witness it is necessary to totally accept Watchtower policy and teaching. It has become increasingly difficult for many Witnesses to harmonise their beliefs with the flood of information that is now available.

Anyone or anything that threatens to upset this delicate balancing act will be avoided totally. For a Witness to even contemplate the possibility that they may not have been told the whole truth is a major step. At stake are not just a set of ideological beliefs, but also the security and protection that the Witness depends upon and maintains by remaining safely within the boundaries that have been set.

Many members are feeling let down and disappointed due to the failure of the promise that a new world would come during the last century. They are bruised and, in some cases, angry. Thousands have left, some after a lifetime of dedicated service. It is essential to respect and sympathise with the situation that the Witness you care for has found his or her self in.

Most Witnesses are principled people who place honesty high on their list of priorities. Appealing to their sense of honesty as a legitimate reason to examine their beliefs, at a pace they can cope with, is a good place to start. Witnesses that find the courage to do this can find that although their conscious minds can make quite rapid changes, their emotional or unconscious minds take far longer to make adjustments. This is true of all people but more so with Witnesses because they have invested so much in their faith.

Once a Witness knows that you are prepared to talk to them about their faith it is best to wait until they approach you then they will be receptive. It is best to register just one thought-provoking point and leave the door open for future conversations. If you are too eager for confrontation you will run into a wall. For a Witness to let you past the wall they have built is an act of trust. That trust must not be betrayed but rewarded by reassuring the Witness that your motives are honourable and that you have their best interests at heart.

As I stated earlier in this book I have avoided listing a number of set ways to debate with a Witness, as those wishing to draw closer to a Witness will fare much better if they follow the guidelines I have suggested and treat each Witness as an individual who has deep feelings for his or her religion.

Life is the only real teacher,
And when books and predictions fail,
It is only then that the true value of loyal friends,
And the love they are able to offer,
Can be fully realized.

✳ ✳ ✳

15

SUMMARY

Careers

Children are encouraged to view pioneering as the only acceptable option when they leave school. Very few pursue further education or plan a career, as planning ahead shows a lack of faith in the world system's imminent end at Armageddon. To strive to achieve any professional position is seen as a compromise. Members are expected to view their secular work as secondary to the promotion of the Watchtower Society. Part-time work is encouraged as this allows more time for Society activity.

Opinions

Witnesses forfeit their right to opinions of their own. All personal interpretation of scripture is forbidden. They are expected to adjust their thinking on all matters to stay in line with the "Faithful and Discreet Slave." To express any doubt about current Society teachings or policy is seen as apostasy. Members are answerable to them for every aspect of their lives; from the type of work they do to how they groom themselves.

Cold Canvassing

All Witnesses are expected to take an active part in calling from door-to-door seeking converts. Funds for such activity come from the restricted efforts of secular work. All such activity is reported and stored on a record card to gauge progress and determine the spirituality of each member. Such reporting is a requirement of baptism, without which there is no salvation. In addition there are three congregation meetings a week to attend, and active participation in these is required.

No Heaven

Everlasting life on earth as a human is the reward promised for faithful service. Members do not believe that all Christians are part of the New Covenant. Only an elect group of 144,000 are believed to go to heaven to rule as kings with Christ. These are said to include the apostles but not the faithful men of old.

The Watchtower Bible & Tract Society

This legally registered corporation states that all interpretation of the Bible has been entrusted to them by their God Jehovah. They state that they are God's only channel of communication with mankind. Despite making numerous false prophecies, they still claim to be God's only true prophet. The Jehovah's Witnesses who make up the membership are told that Jesus has not revealed himself to them personally, but through the Society.

Jehovah Not Jesus

Jehovah's Witnesses are expected to call on the name of Jehovah for salvation, not Jesus. Jesus is seen as an angel, an obedient servant of Jehovah God. He is considered a part of creation and not divine in nature. He is not to be prayed to or worshiped but is just a mediator. There is no salvation without the Watchtower Society who claim to receive their enlightenment directly from Jehovah God.

Friends and Relatives

All relatives, and friends made previous to joining are to be viewed as a threat, in the same way that ancient Israel viewed the surrounding nations. However respectably they live their lives, unless they too join the movement, they are to be avoided socially. This is particularly true if the relatives were once Witnesses but have left the movement. They are believed to

148

have "turned bad." The Society has even advised its members not to open mail if it appears to be from an ex-Witness, even a close relative.

The Watchtower Society has been forced to change the rules concerning relatives a number of times, due to the number of members ignoring their advice and continuing to quietly see those they hold dear. At present there seems to be confusion over what the current ruling is. Although there is no outright ban on having friends who are not Witnesses, doing so is heavily frowned upon, to a point where in reality very few members have friends outside of the organization.

Conditions Of Membership

Many practices are against the Society's law, which if ignored, results in disfellowshipping. Included are the celebration of Birthdays, Christmas, Easter, Mother's Day and Father's Day. Members are not allowed to christen their children, have blood transfusions, smoke or gamble. Higher education and the pursuit of a career are frowned upon. Women are not allowed to hold a position of any kind in their congregation. Door-to-door ministry is compulsory, as is meeting attendance. All members are expected to live by a strict moral code.

No Holy Communion

Jehovah's Witnesses are not allowed to partake of the bread and wine at the Lord's Supper, or Holy Communion, unless they consider themselves to be of the chosen few who hope to live in heaven as kings with Jesus. The membership as a whole, do not believe themselves to be part of the New Covenant which replaced the Old Covenant. They believe that association with other Jehovah's Witnesses is sufficient.

No Other Christians

One of the most disturbing aspects of Jehovah's Witnesses is the way they view all other religions. However sincere others are in their belief and worship, they are accused of belonging to an organization run by the Devil. Professing Christians are considered to be the most evil of all. This is because they claim to be Christ's brothers and sisters. They are considered guilty of distracting people away from the Watchtower Society, in the Witnesses view, the only true religion.

Being a Witness means more than belonging to a section of Christianity. They view themselves as the only Christian group in existence, and will seldom enter church buildings, as the Devil is thought to own them. The Witnesses have judged them and condemned them wholesale. The fact that they believe in and call on the name of Jesus Christ for salvation is not enough in the eyes of a Witness.

16

CONCLUSION

The search for truth has occupied man's thoughts, shaped his dreams, and been the cause of many struggles throughout history. Eternal life has been seen as the ultimate quest since the beginning of time. Religions of the world have sought to show that this goal can only be achieved through belief in a higher being – a supreme spirit.

It is not surprising that a well organized group such as Jehovah's Witnesses, offering a ready made package guaranteed to be "the truth," will appeal to many. They offer everlasting life on earth without surrender of the human body. This is a unique idea, foreign to Christians and most other religions. The idea of once again living on earth with close friends or relatives, who have passed away, is to many an added attraction of this concept.

Faced with the complexity of modern life and the responsibility of making decisions on moral or political issues, many people look for guidance. The Watchtower Society offers this totally. There is a certain feeling of security to be found in an organization that makes all decisions for its members. To be surrounded by people who think the same, share the same goals, hopes and activities, can remove much of the uncertainty in life that many find threatening. These straight mental corridors suit some people but to others they are too restrictive and become a prison.

Some Witnesses join the movement thinking they have at last found the answer to all life's questions, without realising the pressure that will be put on them once involved. Leaving is never easy, especially for those who joined because they felt the need for guidance and help with their lives. Others leave despite thinking they are abandoning "the truth" because they cannot tolerate the regimentation and coercion. They can sometimes carry a feeling of guilt for the rest of their lives. Many try to forget about the idea of a God believing that they are simply not good enough.

It could be said that Jehovah's Witnesses are good people who mean well and try to live up to moral standards they consider to be right. With so many problems in the world why be critical of them?

This study has sought to find whether their claims are true, including their claim that all other Christian and non-Christian sects are evil. A sect that proclaims so loudly to alone have the truth invites examination. Some of the criticisms made, could be applied to other organized religions too. Whether other Christian sects live up to their claims has not been the subject of this study. Whether the Bible itself is consistent is again the subject of a different enquiry.

Jehovah's Witnesses believe that there is a universal court case going on to settle the issue of God's right to rule the earth. The issue is one of universal sovereignty. They claim to be God's witnesses in the court case, appointed by him, to put forward his side of the debate.

If this were a case held even in an imperfect human court, how many times could such witnesses make false statements and claims before their honesty was called into question? How many failed promises and false dates could be entered into the court record before the witnesses were discredited and their testimony considered inadmissible? At what point would the judge conclude that such unreliable testimony was damaging to the case, and such witnesses were actually harming the reputation of the one they were claiming to support?

However well intended the efforts of witnesses in a court case, their testimony has to be truthful and unchanging. It cannot be altered and embellished as the case progresses. It is not enough for the witnesses to say that they meant well and were trying to help. No just court can tolerate such mischief. How well have Jehovah's Witnesses presented their testimony and has it helped the cause of the one they claim has sent them to testify?

152

Jehovah's Witnesses have some of the answers, but to have a share in their lives it is necessary to believe they have all the answers. They are not prepared to be part of the Christian church, contributing their experience and help. The Watchtower Society stands alone and apart from all others, its members must do the same.

Democratic nations have worked and fought for freedom of speech and freedom of worship. Civilised society now demands these freedoms as human rights. The Watchtower Society having fought in the highest courts in the land to defend these freedoms will expel any member who wishes to exercise any degree of freedom. It knows that any Society which allows freedom of expression will inevitably develop a variety of ideas within its structure. A totalitarian leadership cannot survive in such a climate.

The activities of Jehovah's Witnesses are tolerated by society in general because in a free society, people should choose for them-selves how or if they wish to worship. Life is precious only when lived in freedom. Once freedom is lost we become prisoners.

There is, of course, no such thing as total freedom. There are responsibilities and restraints needed for order to exist and to ensure that others rights are respected. But have the Watchtower Society demonstrated the correct way to run a society? Do they have the right to indoctrinate their children into such a narrow cultural mindset? Are they the perfect model for the world to follow, as they claim to be? Do they have knowledge that will lead to everlasting life? Have they dealt with the members in their care in an honest and straightforward way?

It would be unfair and unwise to come to a conclusion having read just my experience. You will have to decide for yourself whether the claims of Jehovah's Witnesses under the leadership of the Watchtower Bible & Tract Society are valid. It is my hope that having learned just a little more of what is behind that knock on your door, you will be more aware when you next open the door to Jehovah's Witnesses and show the necessary caution.

If you are a Witness with doubts who has found the courage to read this far, then I wish you the very best in life and my assurance that there is life beyond the Watchtower Society. If you have a different faith that you are happy with, then treasure it. If you are still searching for answers, then I hope that you will include me among the people who have encouraged you to avoid the short cuts on offer.

The search for truth is a personal responsibility and sometimes the conclusions reached may not be the ones we had hoped for. It is sometimes easier to believe what we want to, rather than face reality. Reality is not always agreeable, but it is always truthful. There is truth in love. There is truth in the silent witness of nature, for it never lies, it simply is and always will be.

Life has chosen to live in you therefore you were worthy of life before you were born. I urge you never to surrender your birthright to gain the approval of those who claim that your right to life is dependent on membership of their club.

You have already been invited to the banquet of life and it is free. The only qualification required is that you are alive – and you are – wonderfully alive.

**I hope that
in your journey
through life
you find peace
within yourself,
for it is the
hallmark
of truth.**

✳ ✳ ✳